The Van Bivi
Logbook

The Van Bivi Logbook

Tales from travels in an Escort Van

Ian Martin

Mountain Lifestyle Publishing
www.mountainlifestyle.co.uk

Copyright © Ian Martin, 2022

All rights reserved. No part of this book may be reproduced or utilised in any form by electronic, mechanical, or other means without prior written permission from the author.

All photos by the author unless otherwise credited.

Printed by KDP

Cover design and layout: Ian Martin
Cover image location: Looe Island, Cornwall

ISBN 9798422302628

On and off the road
Tales from travels in an Escort Van

Down-time, Anglesey, North Wales

For Mo & Dudley

Contents

Introduction 9
Van Life – 2004 15
   Arolla, Switzerland 17
Van Life 2005 23
   Valais, Switzerland 25
   Saas-Fee, Switzerland 33
   Verbier, Switzerland 37
   Grindelwald, Switzerland 40
   Interlaken, Switzerland 44
   Zinal, Switzerland 45
   Finale Ligure, Italy 49
   Finale, Italy 53
   Gran Paradiso, Italy 55
   Chamonix, France 57
   Chamonix, France 61
   Chateau D'Oex, Switzerland 62
   Kernow, England 65
   Talland Bay, Cornwall 67
   Llangollen, Wales 69
   Land's End, Cornwall 71
   Llangollen, Wales 73
Van Life – 2006 75
   Ladock, Cornwall 77
   Cornwall, England 78
   Bude, Cornwall 80
   St Agnes, Cornwall 81
   St Agnes, Cornwall 83
Van Life – 2007 85
   Bala, North Wales 87

 Metz, France 90

 Mojstrana, Slovenia 97

 Mojstrana, Slovenia 99

 West Coast, Croatia 102

 Paklenica, Croatia 104

 Paklenica, Croatia 106

 Osp, Slovenia 108

 Trieste, Italy 110

 Northern Italy 112

 Saint-Omer, France 116

Van Life – 2008 117

 Troyes, France 118

 Cormot, France 120

 Fontainebleau, France 121

 Boulogne, France 122

 Torpoint, Cornwall 123

 Rouen, France 124

 Picos de Europa, Spain 125

 Fuente Dé, Spain 131

 Picos de Europa, Spain 134

 Hossegor, France 140

Afterword 145

Further Van Logbook Entries 147

About the Author 159

Further Reading 161

Introduction

So, what is a 'bivi' anyway?

A bivi (or 'bivouac'), is generally regarded by outdoor types as some form of improvised shelter or 'a campsite of a temporary nature'. They are often undertaken by people who are travelling light in the mountains, but the term 'van bivi' is one we coined to refer to times when we spent a night sleeping in the back of our Ford Escort Van. Sometimes these nights out 'in the wilds' were planned affairs, while others were a last-minute solution to needing somewhere horizontal to sleep in an unforeseen situation or circumstance. As you might expect, the level of comfort and enjoyment on any bivi, be it mountainside or roadside, can usually be directly correlated to the amount of prior knowledge and planning that has been involved.

Generally, for me and Clare (Clare being my girlfriend and later my wife as the travels and years progressed), a van bivi was a planned night away. Afterwards, having enjoyed, survived, or sometimes just endured the night, notes were documented in a small hardback book which was kept in the back of the van. These notes have since provided both a point of reference for future travels as well as a historical record of (often comedic) events.

The van has accompanied us on many more adventures than are documented in this book because while on longer van travels we would often pitch a tent to sleep in, using the back of the van as a kitchen and lounge for the evening. However, those evenings and nights out were not documented in the official 'van bivi book', which is why locations listed on the contents page seem to jump around a bit. So, although we've spent months and months travelling across Europe with the van over the years, to make it into the official 'logbook' record and therefore become a story documented here, we had to actually sleep in the van.

As well as logbooks I also keep expedition diaries and it was while searching for some information in one of them that I came across the original 'Van Bivi Logbook'. I couldn't resist dusting it off and having a flick through it. Before I knew what was happening, I'd lost an hour and had been transported back to all sorts of places and reminded of many crazy events that I'd long since forgotten about. It seemed a shame to have such adventures hidden away in a scrawled notebook gathering dust, so they've been transcribed here for your reading pleasure, along with additional details to paint a picture in your mind of some of our travels and explorations around Europe at the start of the century in our Ford Escort van.

Why a Ford Escort Van?

The Escort is the thread that links these far-fetched tales of travel, companionship and adventure. It was just an inconspicuous, small, white builder's van. Nothing flashy or with cause to draw the eye; just a discrete little van that to the casual observer bears no trace of its ability to house its owners on so many adventures. I ended up as the owner of the Escort due to circumstance rather than a strong pull towards this specific make or model. To be fair, it's not the obvious choice of vehicle for the travels I had in mind, but it is one that served us well for many years.

Having been through university without owning a vehicle, I had been consciously (and I suspect also unconsciously), taking notes and observations of other climbers, travellers and van dwellers, picking up on the pros and cons of various makes, models, designs and out-fittings. After graduating, a vehicle was going to be required for both my choices of work and leisure. Weighing up the options (despite having never actually seen one used in the way I intended to), the Escort seemed to fit my initial criteria, availability and most critically, my budget.

When I say, 'fitted my budget', I never actually had enough money to buy the van outright (or any van for that matter) until many years later. But I did have some financially savvy parents, who presented me with some options for 'finding' the required cash, without disappearing into a deep hole of inescapable debt. By taking advantage of the boom in the new wave of introductory credit-card offers (before the Financial Services Authority began to crack down on them) I was able to purchase the van on a newly signed up credit-card deal, where I was granted a very generous twelve months of interest-free credit on my first purchase. It looked like, and was, a great deal, providing you repaid the balance before a staggeringly inflated interest rate was applied. For the unaware, the scheme was a carefully laid trap that created nightmares, but with care, it could be advantageously negotiated.

Twelve months of enjoyable van travel later, when the borrowed purchase price needed to be repaid, I transferred the balance to a new credit card company, who were offering the same deal for any 'balance transfers'. This process was repeated over and over until the crazy 'interest-free' credit deals began to die out. During this time, I'd diligently been saving up enough money to be able to pay off the initial debt, so that eventually I owned the van outright, having borrowed the money interest-free for about seven years. It required a bit of planning to make sure that a new card provider was sourced and lined up every time, but it did mean that I was able to purchase the van, despite having no money to initially buy it with. This kickstarted my van travelling career as well as my financial education.

Even to the most ardent of fans, the Ford Escort is a far cry from the luxurious, spacious campervans that we would often (and I'll admit, sometimes enviously), admire while parked up in the shadow of on our travels. Owning a campervan, when you are going camping or travelling is clearly the superior choice, but for much of the ordinary and necessary day to day travel that I was also going to require, the practicalities and economy of a small van made it a better choice. So, we took the shell of a second-hand builder's van, swept out the spilt sand and cement, buffed up the dusty dashboard and added in what luxuries we could.

Van Transformation

For anyone who has attempted to turn a builder's van into a comfortable place to rest their head, you'll appreciate the details of the van transformation. I was, of course, on a tight budget so everything was sourced from my Dad's garage, which is well stocked due to a lifetime in the building industry. His trademark motto of "it will come in handy one day" was finally justified.

The first job involved removing the in-situ wooden panels which lined the interior and stuffing insulation behind them to soundproof and increase interior warmth. Over the years, the plywood walls would become decorated with a bright pattern of stickers that provided travel mementoes from all sorts of campsites, events and products. The ceiling was then covered with a thin foam lining which helped to deaden sound and reduce condensation. After a rummage in the roof of my Dad's garage, we had a selection of carpet off-cuts to go on the floor. The best bit was 'L' shaped but wasn't quite big enough to cover the whole floor. However, in a stroke of good fortune, we managed to couple it with a small square of lino which we put at the back for storing wet kit or muddy boots on. Before laying the flooring, we added several layers of insulation and cushioning using old foam Karrimats that I'd accumulated from various past expeditions.

Curtains, of a let's say 'retro' style, originally from my parent's first house, were hung between the cab and the back. The brown flowered pattern of the thick material did a great job of maintaining privacy and keeping out the light while sleeping. In certain circles, I'm sure they could be considered a genuine mix of vintage fashion and function.

The only fixed storage area was a plywood box, neatly finished with a classy dark hardwood trim that ran along the right-hand side of the van. It was sturdy enough to sit on and inside there was space for basic cooking equipment and other random 'van essentials'. The box lid doubled up as a makeshift table for al-fresco cooking and dining by balancing it between the back bumper and two full climbing rucksacks placed outside the back of the van. When sleeping, all our bags were piled onto the front seats and two Therm-a-Rest mattresses slotted perfectly together alongside the plywood box.

At the end of the box near the rear doors, was a small space that was reserved for the 'library' of climbing guidebooks. These were loaned from friends or taken from our ever-expanding guidebook collection. The only resident book was, of course, the *'Van Bivi Logbook'*. While the logbook recorded the dates and details of each overnight stay, a tally was etched on the wood panelling behind the driver.

We didn't install a leisure battery for the van so lighting mostly came from battery-powered LED lamps that clipped to the ceiling. We also had a few candle lanterns that gave great ambience, as well as a small fire extinguisher and fire blanket mounted nearby, just in case.

Various hooks, clips and bungees were utilised to maximise the efficiency of storage space along the top edges and ceiling of the van. For extended travel trips, other ingenious attachments and additions were invented or created, such as the wok, which was held fast to the left-hand wall in a web-like grip of elasticated strips. On a previous tent-based expedition in the Arctic, to make sure you could always find a lighter for the stove, we fixed it to the tent wall using a strip of sticky-backed Velcro. Employing the same tried and tested technique in the van, a lighter could always be found attached to the back wall.

In the front, apart from the brown flowery curtains, it looked like an ordinary van. There were no distinguishing markings on the outside to suggest that there could be two people asleep in the back. 'In-flight entertainments' were provided from the radio/cassette player and later, through a mega upgrade via an adapter, a state of the art iPod Nano. Air conditioning came in the form of 'winding down the window' and navigation was conducted using a good old fashioned road map under the close watch of the occupier of the passenger seat.

Setting the Scene

Now that you've been introduced to the concept of the 'Van Bivi' and the Escort van, which became fondly known as 'The Cessna', let me help to set the scene for this book. It begins in 2004, having just taken on a position in Switzerland, working as an expedition leader and outdoor education teacher for a private school in the French-speaking Caton of Vaud.

Filled with a selection of outdoor gear and most of my personal belongings, I made the arduous solo journey (Clare joined me a few weeks later) from Wales to Switzerland. Crossing the channel, the van was one of only two vehicles occupying the slightly spooky late-night ferry crossing. Then onwards through the flat interior of France, the van transported me into the spectacular and magical vistas of the Swiss Alps. Driving nervously up the last switchback to our new alpine residence at an altitude of 1200m, with sweaty hands gripping the steering wheel tightly, it seemed unlikely at the time that the little van would ever make it back in one piece. But as you'll see in this book, The Cessna stood the test of time as both a launch pad and basecamp to many a fine adventure.

For consistency and in keeping with the original logbook, each story begins with the name of the place and country of the van bivi, a description of the area, the date of the bivi and the original logbook entry.

The accompanying stories provide a flavour of the adventures that The Cessna provided a base for, along with a little reminiscing about additional antics in faraway lands. Feel free to read the book cover to cover, or simply dip into a place that sounds most interesting to you.

Anyone could do what we have done, but most people don't. We haven't necessarily climbed the hardest rock climbs, skied the steepest couloirs or summited the highest peaks, but we have been consistently out there, making the most of what we have to create authentic explorations of our own. Operating with a modest budget, we've enjoyed using our skills to seek out adventures. This book is a collection of stories to document, inspire and motivate us (and perhaps you) to keep the adventures coming.

Van Life – 2004

Arriving back at base after a Ski Tour, North Wales

Arolla, Switzerland
By the woods on the edge of the village

October 16th 2004

LOGBOOK ENTRY:
"A high-altitude winter bivi. Cold enough to freeze the diesel!"

How cold could it be anyway? We'd done this kind of thing before, in fact, we'd become rather good at it. Escapades such as the one we found ourselves on required a comfortable and affordable home for the night and the Cessna, as our little van was known, seemed to fit the bill nicely. Having served a loyal apprenticeship on numerous beaches, riverbanks, valleys and crag bases across England, Wales and Scotland, the time had come to test its mettle against the mighty Alps.

The small Alpine region of Arolla is nestled high on the western side of the Swiss alpine region known as Valais. Leaving the flatlands and security of the Rhone Valley, we headed up the ever-steepening road, rapidly dropping gears as we navigated the turns. The scenery was spectacular and was a constant source of driver distraction as we revved our way up countless zig-zags and switchbacks, to where the road finally ended at Arolla. We were going to say in the village of Arolla and I'm sure that during the height of both the summer and winter seasons, it's a bustling hub of activity full of tourists, mountaineers and skiers. Presently though, it had a real ghost town feel to it with chalets closed for the off-season and empty campsites that didn't entice us in. In the village square, there was a vague sense of civilization; a shop was open and there was a telephone box too. Luckily, the shopkeeper could understand my broken, stuttering French and was prepared to sell us a map and a phone card. A purchase which made us feel better on two counts. We could now check that we were where we thought we were and could also contact the outside world should we need to, without having to incur the vast expense of using our mobile phone.

A short reconnaissance around the sunny streets and surrounding area revealed a perfectly placed car park below the edge of the forest, idyllically positioned by a small stream. This was set to serve as our alpine base camp. Despite the dismal forecast, the weather was glorious, and sunshine streamed into the back of the van as we brewed up hot chocolates on the stove. After consulting our newly acquired map and climbing guidebook, we decided that it was a bit late in the day to be heading off into the mountains. We had hoped to walk up to an alpine hut and then climb a peak the following day. These huts have a resident warden during the summer months but are left uninhabited during the winter until the ski touring season begins. They generally all have a 'winter room' left unlocked during the colder off-season months, so that mountaineers have somewhere to take shelter, but we didn't know for sure if this one did or not. We had time to get to the hut, but after a bit of discussion decided that we didn't fancy taking the risk, as if it was locked, we would have to journey back in the dark, on what was promising to be a cold night; a prospect that neither of us particularly relished.

And so it was, that we decided to go on an acclimatisation trek above the village. The distance we actually covered was minimal as most of the time was spent taking photos of the stunning scenery, checking our bearings and identifying the surrounding peaks on the newly acquired map. The views were splendid. Above the green of the valley floor, the larches were turning orangey-red and were sprinkled with a dusting of freshly fallen snow. The air was crisp and fresh - cold enough to numb our noses, but when the sun shone through the passing clouds, the warmth felt life-giving.

On arrival back at basecamp (the van), we set about turning the van from travel mode into bivi mode – a careful process of stacking bags and equipment to allow us to fit in amongst it all. By the time we'd brewed our first hot chocolate, the sun had dropped below the horizon and with it, the temperature. It suddenly became clear that it was going to be a rather cold night and much colder than we'd perhaps anticipated. Preparations for the evening meal were undertaken inside the van in full hat, gloves and down jacket armour. Unfortunately, to get the best use of available light, we had to cook with the back door open which ensured that what little heat the gas stove produced, was quickly and efficiently ushered outside, thus making the difference between temperatures inside and outside the van negligible. Once darkness had crept up the valley, we shut the door and wrapped ourselves in our sleeping bags, continuing our meal preparations by torchlight.

The joys of hot food inside a hungry cold body are one of the simple pleasures that expeditioners relish. It's like filling up a machine before or after use and is essential to performance and morale. Having the veritable luxury of the van and its utensils, meant that we were able to rustle up a delightful feast of sausages, veggies and pasta. Having spent so long cooking the meal, the results were demolished in a disproportionate amount of time as the night seemed to be sucking away the heat from the food almost immediately after it was taken off the stove.

We cleared away our cooking kit as tidily and quickly as possible, although it took some time due to us working as much as we could with our gloves on. The temperature outside, before we shut the door had been minus seven degrees Celsius and it looked like it was going to get much colder before it got any warmer. Once packed away we got fully inside our bags to conserve the little heat that each of us possessed. Time passed very quickly as we nattered away and planned our future fortunes. Just before sleep took over, we popped outside into a brilliant starry night for a final look around. I would have loved to have stayed outside longer to observe the night sky but could feel the heat literally falling off me and my survival instincts and common sense told me to get back inside. It was time for bed.

Thank heavens for down sleeping bags. Despite drifting in and out of consciousness a few times in the night, I woke feeling refreshed and toasty inside my sleeping bag. However, before I'd even lifted an eyelid or had begun to remember where I was, I could sense the sub-par temperatures around me. Sometimes after a night in the van, a small amount of condensation would gather on the ceiling and the first thing that struck me when I opened my eyes was that last night's condensation was no longer condensation at all - it was now a thick frost, complete with little icicles hanging from it. It wasn't just on the ceiling either; anywhere that wasn't insulated and was bare metal, was covered in frosty ice. We were sleeping inside a freezer!

Having got dressed while still inside our sleeping bags, we opened the back door to find that a few centimetres of fresh snow had fallen during the night. Although the sky now contained only a scattering of clouds it would be at least a few hours until the sun hit the van, as the high mountains that surrounded us kept us in the shade. We weren't the only ones that were feeling the cold that morning. Despite being kept inside my sleeping bag overnight, the gas stove protested about being stuck out in the snow and refused to roar in its usual comforting way. Instead, it slowly coughed and spluttered, taking over half an hour to boil enough water for us to have a coffee. Despite the wait, the restorative brew was well received and boosted both morale and body temperatures. Both of which were going to be essential for our enjoyment of the day.

Slowly but surely, we began to get organised and packed up for some alpine antics. Clare carefully picked the icicles off the ceiling while I brushed the snow off the van and by the time we were ready to set off, the sun was upon us which meant that the van had started to defrost. We set off on foot towards the remote cabin, which was located some seven kilometres away. Although it was not too far, it was going to be no walk in the park, with the journey containing about a thousand metres of height gain, as well as a glacier and high col crossing before we would reach it.

Just before we arrived at the col that would lead us down to where we needed to cross the glacier, snowflakes started falling. The weather had been getting steadily worse since our departure from the van, with the clouds slowly turning darker and becoming bigger. Before long, we were enveloped in a Scottish style blizzard of whiteout conditions. The field of vision which had started the day as several kilometres was now reduced to only a few metres. Not ideal for locating a small cabin on a large mountainside.

Coming across a suitably large boulder that could just about accommodate us in its lee, we paused for a team talk. We huddled there for a few minutes, devouring our sandwiches and considering the options. Before too long, it became apparent that the only sane option for us was to head back to base camp. But rather than retrace our steps, we opted to continue until we could join a path that would take us on a circular walk back to the van. Apart from the sighting of a small herd of Chamois, the return journey passed without major incident. The major incident was to happen once we got back to the van! Despite crossed fingers and much coaxing, The Cessna just wouldn't start. We tried until the battery went flat and then started pushing in hope of a bump start, all to no avail.

We pulled off the road into another layby. The temperature at this point was hovering around zero, so the first thing we did was put on all our spare clothes. While Clare set about brewing hot drinks, I phoned the breakdown service on the emergency mobile. To save our phone bill, they volunteered to phone us back and I eagerly accepted the offer. While we waited for their call, I decided to be proactive and got out the jump leads in the hope of someone passing by and stopping to help.

Given that we were near the end of a dead-end road, our luck was in, as someone did stop. Better than just stopping, they also seemed to have a bit of knowledge about the workings of a diesel combustion engine - something that is sorely lacking in my education. After several jump-start attempts, the kind stranger concluded that the battery was fine and that the problem was something else. Oh dear, we thought. Our concern must have been clear, so taking pity on us, he then phoned his friend who lived nearby to see if he could make a more productive diagnosis. In due course, another car pulled into the layby to assist the stranded foreigners. A glance under the bonnet was all it took for him to come up with the solution.

Working like a couple of surgeons, the two began to unscrew and move aside different parts of the engine. By this time the hot drinks were brewed and the mechanic/surgeon motioned us to pass the stove. This, he positions against the fuel pump and told us to stand back as he sparked it up! As we nervously glanced over, the other guy got into the cockpit and attempted to start the van. After a few minutes, it came so close to making some encouraging noises, but just as it was about to roar into life the battery died again. We quickly connected our battery to theirs and a little while later the van spluttered into life. The next five minutes were spent revving the van like it's never been revved before. Clouds and clouds of thick smoke poured out of the exhaust blackening the ground all around, but it had started and that was such a relief. We felt so grateful to our two saviours.

As our rescuers returned to the warmth of their chalets, we set the navigation system to head for home and waved goodbye to the mountains. Trundling off down the hill, it was only two hours later that we arrived back in the warmth of our own home. Who knows how long it would have taken for the breakdown service to have found us? Would they have even come looking for us on a Sunday? Luckily, we didn't have to find out and incidentally, they still haven't phoned back.

Van Life 2005

Post-climb relaxation, Aosta Valley, Italy

Valais, Switzerland
Service Station Car Park on the E62 (Westbound)

March 21st 2005

LOGBOOK ENTRY:
"Having completed a successful ascent and ski descent of the Wildstrubel (3243.5m), a retreat was made directly to the thermal baths of Leukerbad (a place of unaffordable luxury and relaxation, made accessible to us, only via a discount ticket that we had been given). However, unfortunately, the experience has relaxed us so much that we were unable to stay awake for the journey home and had to make an emergency bivi in the back of the van at the motorway services between Sion and Martigny. The following day we mounted an ambitious attempt on the Dent du Morcle, which ended in a blizzard retreat some distance from the summit".

We had been living in Switzerland since the previous summer and as soon as the first snow had fallen, we had taken every opportunity to travel on skis whenever we could. This turned out to be rather a lot. At the weekends, I was working with students either on ski touring or snowshoeing courses and expeditions, but during the weekdays we generally had limited commitments and the Swiss Alps at our disposal. The only thing we lacked was the funds to travel too far afield. Our local lift passes gave us access to a huge amount of ski terrain, but the expense of staying in the high mountain huts was out of our weekly budget. This meant that day tours, usually in the local area, became our speciality. All told, we spent nearly 100 days on skis that winter, with the majority involving a ski tour of some sort.

Though the details of exactly how or why escape me now, we had been given a discount pass to the faraway thermal bath resort of Leukerbad. I think it was assumed that we'd never be able to afford to go, yet as part of our Swiss inductions, we were told that we really ought to have experienced it. Whatever the reason, we eventually got around to planning an excuse to be in the area. The Wildstrubel, as well as being a finely named peak, looked to be an excellent ski tour that was conveniently in the vicinity of the delightful thermal destination. On closer inspection, if we were going to travel all that way and ascend such a lofty peak, we were going to have to splash out on a night's accommodations at the conveniently placed Lammerenhutte. Perhaps a few other peaks could even be included in the itinerary? Swiss francs were counted up, weather forecasts checked and the van was fuelled, loaded and deemed ready for an adventure.

We lived in an idyllic ski village with a picture-postcard Swiss mountain landscape, wooden chalets, cows with bells and all the other stereotypical trimmings. But there was still a desire to escape the village at times, so we made the 10 km descent to the Rhone Valley which was marked by a steady increase in temperature. It was always a bit of a shock travelling from one season to another just by heading into the valley. The winter still held its grip on the village which was hemmed in by jagged snowy peaks and littered with ski lifts, but in contrast, the organised, lush green fields and vineyards of the lower valley bore no trace of snow and the spring flowers were in full bloom. It was as if we'd been transported into another world.

Once down in the wide-open flatlands, we followed the main road on the gloriously level tarmac towards Martigny, where the natural turn in direction was dictated by the topography, having been carved out by some ancient glaciers. Down here, on the textbook flat bottom of the U-shaped valley, the Escort van and its driver would both always heave a sigh of relief. It had not taken long after arriving in Switzerland to discover that mighty mountain passes, and steep switch-back roads were not going to be the van's forte. On the way uphill, the temperature gauge would rise like an altimeter, as we repetitively switched from first to second gear. While we coaxed it upwards, the road behind us would slowly clog up with traffic, and impatient drivers would periodically scream past with high revs at the briefest glimpse of a section of straight road. Then there were the downhills, efficient on fuel, but detrimental to the life of the brake pads. The time taken to drive up or down a pass was almost always equal, as was the wear on van parts and nerves.

Anticipation, ambition, and excitement were a heady mix as we made our way up to another 'new area'. We had ticked our way through a good deal of the suggested ski itineraries in our local guidebook, but this trip would take us into a completely new canton. Although by now, we were relatively competent ski tourers rapidly gaining experience, we knew our chosen agenda involved some glacier crossings and with this comes an extra element of required skill and equipment. At this time of year, most of the crevasses would be covered or filled with snow, but it was still something that needed to be considered and prepared for. Our local skiing area was low enough not to have any glaciated terrain, which gave us a lot more freedom of route choice as well as the advantage of having to carry less equipment. But there's something about travelling by ski in the high mountains in glacial terrain. It requires an extra level of alertness and the need to tune into the environment. To be up close and among the jumbling masses of rock and ice is a humbling experience and demands respect as well as knowledge for safe passage. Our chosen tour was to follow a fairly standard route up to a high mountain hut, via an ascent of the nearby Daubenhorn. Here we would rest for the night, before making a summit bid on the Wildstrubel the next morning.

Having parted with an eye-watering amount of cash at the lift station, we began the smooth ride upwards in the cable car, transporting ourselves, in a few short minutes back into the familiar world of snow and ice. For the purest mountaineer, using the mechanical uplift could be seen as cheating, but we were more than happy to watch the altimeter on my watch tick upwards without having to exert any energy. From the top of the lift, we crossed easily over the Gemipass and made our way gently up the open valley of the Lamerenboden. Using the lift system may give quick and easy access, but the sudden arrival into wild terrain does sometimes give a culture shock of sorts. The sight and sound of the mechanics and crowds were soon left behind and an eerie quiet descended. As we set off, a parallel set of ski tracks in the snow were the only evidence of other human interference.

The few other ski tourers who had set their sights on a similar objective soon thinned out as we all found our natural paces. With the weather looking settled, we had no cause to rush, so we were able to relax into the steady melodic groove of skinning up the valley. The skins made a satisfying 'swish' as they were guided forward across the frozen surface of the snow while rhythmically aligned with the 'clack' of the heel bindings connecting with the ski between steps.

If you've never ski toured before, then let me explain a few things that will make this read a little easier to picture. To ascend uphill by ski, a 'skin' is applied to the base of our skis. Originally, this would have been made using a seal skin, but these days a much more convenient velvet-like strip, with an adhesive backing, is used. Stretching along the length of the ski, it's stuck down and clipped to the tip of the ski. The skins allow the ski to be slid or pushed uphill, in a forward motion. A backwards slip is prevented by the material gripping the surface of the snow. Imagine stroking a cat or a thick velvet cushion - it only works in one direction! These skins, when coupled with a special type of ski binding that allows the heel of one's boot to lift, mean that the user can 'shuffle' forwards in a relatively efficient way. Once mastered, it soon becomes clear that this is 'the' way to travel in the high mountains in winter. The ski also spreads the weight of the skier across the snow, preventing them from sinking too deep should the snow be soft and powdery. Of course, the snowshoe offers a similar solution to travel across deep snow, but with skinning on skis, the best part of the day begins at the summit, whereas the snowshoer still has a long plod home!

The ascent of the Daubenhorn (2941m) was made without incident and the summit was gained with the assistance of a fast team up ahead putting in a good track. After delighting in having the summit to ourselves we enjoyed a steady, yet cautious ski down the northwest slopes, where a final transition back into uphill mode got us up to the hut and brought an end to the day's excursions.

The weather was fabulous, with high pressure keeping the alpine skies brilliantly bright. Along with a few other ski tourers, we sat out on the hut terrace, basking in the afternoon sunshine among a colourful array of socks, skins, boots and inners which had been laid out to dry. As far as the eye could see and in every direction were snow-covered peaks and I spent some time trying to identify our 'local' ones in the far distance.

The hut had a resident guardian which added the extra luxury (and of course, expense) of having an evening meal and breakfast provided. To add some clarity, when I say Hut, I'm actually in this instance, talking about a three-story high, relatively modern, well-insulated Swiss mountain chalet. On arrival, having checked in with the guardian, we were told where to leave our skis, bags and boots, given a pair of 'hut slippers' then assigned a place on the communal bunk bed. These 'alpine bunks' are designed to ensure maximum occupancy within the limited dimensions of a mountain hut. Two or three platforms each accommodate anything up to about ten people, with a pillow and blanket or duvet provided. Personal belongings must be stored in a basket outside of the dorm. The aim of this is to reduce the amount of rustling and rucksack faff while others are sleeping and to be fair, with barely a metre wide corridor between the bunks, there's hardly any space for them anyway.

Sleeping in a communal dorm like this doesn't usually rate highly on anyone's 'top ten sleeps' list and for good reason. Even though most of the inhabitants climb into their bunks well fed and in a general state of fatigue (having all had to have made the physically taxing ascent to the hut in the first place), having twenty or so bed-mates all quiet and still at the same time seems beyond the realms of possibility. For a start, it takes a while for everyone to go to bed. Those with the biggest day ahead of them, along with those who've had the biggest day today, retire first. The latter can usually be distinguished by the degree of sunburn on their faces, the thickness of sunblock on their lips and a look of vacant dehydration. And of course, by smell. At the other end of the spectrum, some groups are roaring with laughter, sociably knocking back red wine by the carafe, seemingly impervious to the impacts of the altitude or their wallets. The others in between these two groups are just busy packing.

Often, packing involves searching for your kit among a jumble of ice axes and identical-looking ski boots. Then having located everything, and stashed it in your basket, you remember that your head torch or toothbrush is at the bottom of the sack and the repacking starts again. Or maybe that's just me? Once inside the (by now dark) dorm room, the first trick is to remember which section of the bunk is yours. The seasoned alpinist will already have their head torch on them and will have laid out a sleeping bag liner and a water bottle as a marker of their territory. Having identified your spot and perhaps reclaimed your pillow from a cheeky nearby resident, the fun of getting undressed inside your liner begins.

Remember that this of course needs to be done without disturbing the mattress too much, without shining a light in someone's eyes and needs to finish with yourself being well tucked in under your blanket and still within your 'zone'. And of course, you will also have managed to leave your 'hut slippers' somewhere close at hand, to be able to relocate them in the morning - no easy feat, given that they look exactly the same as everyone else's!

At this point, having successfully got yourself horizontal without elbowing the stranger next to you in the face or hitting your head on the bunk above, somebody usually wants the window open. More often than not, the combined resident body heat ensures that it's stiflingly hot in the dorm and all attempts to have hydrated during the evening quickly begin to sweat away. But shortly after breathing the life-saving cool air of the crisp alpine night into your lungs, somebody usually gets up to close it. Sometimes there is a bit of grumbling in a foreign language, and sometimes not. Someone always needs a pee in the night, which almost certainly means your hut slippers will be gone by the morning. Someone's tossing and turning. Someone sleep talks and of course, there is always at least one unsociably loud snorer.

Earplugs are seen as essential as sunglasses and sun cream up here. But luckily for me, that is not something that I have to worry about packing. Having unwittingly cultivated an enormous brain tumour and survived the subsequent removal of it in my early twenties, one side effect was being left with only one working ear. While this is extremely confusing and disorientating in a noisy room, in an alpine bunk scenario, the one-eared sleeper is king. With my 'good ear' laid restfully down on a pillow, I'm as good as deaf. While this is certainly a virtue when it comes to bedtime, it does have its limitations when it comes to waking up. As a result, Clare is usually in charge of alarm calls and the task of bringing me back into consciousness.

High up in a mountain hut, there are plenty more factors at play when it comes to getting a good night's sleep than just some peace and quiet. The day ahead is being planned out and rehearsed in my mind, usually with a decent degree of caution and quite often with a sizable dose of worry as well. What will the weather be like tomorrow? Is it clouding over? Snowing? Do I know where all my kit is? Did I bring my boots inside? Am I hydrated enough? Do I need to pee? What is Plan B? What's our turnaround time? What if it's too windy/cloudy/cold/warm/hard/tiring? The list goes on, but eventually sleep arrives to allow some actual rest.

Breakfast time in a hut is usually pre-arranged with the Guardian the night before and can be whenever you request. It's not uncommon for alarms to start beeping at 3 or 4 am for those with big objectives, but ours was a respectable 6 am. The unsociably early starts are a necessity rather than an actual preference and are usually made to increase the margins of safety on the mountain, rather than simply for the challenge of forcing your body to accept some stale bread and sweet coffee while it still wants to be sleeping. Safe travel across certain parts of mountains or glaciers requires the snow to be frozen, which is more likely in the cool of the morning, hence the early 'alpine start'. While the hardship of leaving a warm and happy slumber to stagger into the icy darkness of an alpine morning takes some amount of motivation, it is at least, usually rewarded with the visual euphoria of witnessing the alpine dawn.

Setting off by headtorch, under the star-studded skies is the warm-up (literally as well as metaphorically), for the coming light show. Navigation is helped by the bluish tinge in the east, which gradually brightens, while the peaks in the west begin to glow pink in the warmth of the coming light. As the stars fade away and the skies turn to pale blue, the expectant finale comes as the sun bursts over the horizon, casting long shadows that shuffle along next to you amid a sea of sparkling snow crystals.

Often referred to by photographers as 'the golden hour', this magical time repeats itself just before sunset, in reverse order. For me, it's a time of heightened senses and always instils a sense of true awe and wonder, especially in such mountainous terrain. On this particular morning, we were approaching the short but steeper crevassed zone as the first warming rays of illuminating light touched the glacier. Before ascending to our high point for the day, we detoured slightly to take in the lower peak of Mittlegipfel (3242m), then continued onwards to the main summit of the Wildstrubel. Surprisingly, the final few paces over the wide summit to the crowning cross were completely devoid of snow. We tottered over the rocky ground in our ski boots for an obligatory photograph and to sign our names in the 'summit book' which was housed in a box on the side of an enormous wooden cross.

The view was hard to take in. Dramatic peaks jostled for competition along a full three-sixty-degree panorama as far as the eyes could see, while below us the oddly level ground of the Glacier de la Pleine Mort looked strangely out of place. It was a fine spot to be enjoying a bit of food and nice to be off the skis while allowing the satisfying relief of being on top to wash over us. As I mentioned earlier, if we'd hiked up here with snowshoes, we'd still have a big job on our hands getting safely back down to the hut. But with our skins removed from our skis and bindings clipped into 'downhill' mode, all we had to do was let gravity assist our descent as we put in slow long curving turns.

The snow was still quite firm, but the sun had softened the top layer enough to give some great spring skiing conditions. Keeping our uphill tracks in view, we made our descent using long traversing pitches. This had the advantage of getting maximum ski time for our uphill efforts but also meant that we didn't have to make too many difficult tight turns, which we weren't exactly super skilled at.

It can seem a disappointing ratio of time spent skinning uphill versus the time it takes to slide back down again, but it almost always leaves you with a feeling that it has been well worth the effort. After navigating our way to the glacier, being sure to give the crevassed zones a particularly wide berth, we didn't bother crossing back over to the hut. Instead, we continued our descent down to the Gemipass where the lift awaited. Taking one last look at the wilderness of snow and ice, we climbed aboard and were smoothly transported at an ear-popping speed back into the hustle and bustle below.

As the village came into focus, we were pressed up against the window of the cable car, soaking in the view. Below us, we could see the steaming blue waters of the open-air thermal baths. Despite there being some snow around the pool, people were walking around in shorts and bikinis in the afternoon sunshine. We couldn't get there fast enough! With skis safely stashed in the van and boots replaced with comfy trainers, we checked into a world of luxury and set about exploring the new terrain of saunas, steam rooms, jacuzzies, ice rooms and all manner of pools, both indoors and out. In between discovering a new area, we'd drink water and lie back on one of the many loungers that were never far from reach. We'd descended some 2000m from a remote, cold, high alpine peak and landed here in a hot tub. It was a lot to take in mentally and physically!

Having set off pre-dawn, it was no surprise really that once we'd left the spa and driven as far as the valley floor, we both felt ruinously tired. It was quite a combination for anybody to take on - hard exertion at cold altitudes, followed up with hot temperatures in a low altitude relaxing environment. Coupled with an early start and the previous day's ascent to the hut, it was probably a bit ambitious to think we'd be fine to drive a few hours back home. With skis hoisted up into the roof of the van, we nestled quietly into our sleeping bags among a mass of kit with even less room to manoeuvre than the night before. It was a tight little space, but it was our little space and unlike in the hut, sleep came quickly and easily.

Saas-Fee, Switzerland
Ski Area Car Park

March 24th 2005

LOGBOOK ENTRY:
"In order to save an early start from home, we had thought of camping in the car park at Saas-Fee, so that we could attempt an ascent of the Allalinhorn (4027m). In the end though, we opted for the comfy bed and the alpine start from home. However, now totally exhausted from our efforts, we are indeed parked next to Pete Rowland's Transit (aka Air Force One), in said car park, but he and Dave are currently staying up at a hut somewhere".

The Allalinhorn is a big peak. With a height of 4027m it only just qualifies as one of the 82 coveted summits that stand over the height of 4000m, but it is still a sizeable mass of a mountain. While generally considered to be a good entry-level peak in terms of ski touring objectives in the bigger mountains, it is still a serious undertaking. To be fair, doing anything at 4000m meters feels like a serious undertaking. Just getting a breath into your lungs and oxygen into the bloodstream can seem like a hard-won battle. And that's without the added exertion involved in climbing a mountain - especially on a set of skis in sub-zero temperatures.

Acclimatisation to altitude is a key requisite for both safety and enjoyment and this takes time to achieve. As we'd been living at a reasonable altitude for a while and had now spent a few days 'up high' at around 3500m, it seemed like a good idea to capitalize on this physiological advantage that we'd gained and take the next step up, over the 4000m barrier. It's not that either of us was fixed on climbing a 4000m peak, or the Allalinhorn in particular, it was just that we were fit and acclimatised, so thought we ought to make the most of it and the Allalinhorn was billed as a 'good one to go for'.

I'd climbed some of the big peaks in the Saas Valley on a previous summer trip back in 1999, but not the Allalinhorn, so part of me was keen to go back to see if I remembered much of it and add a new summit to my tally. Saas-Fee is a car-free village high up in the Valais Canton of the Swiss Alps. Having coaxed the van up the never-ending switch-backed approach, we came to rest in the main car park at the limit of motorised vehicle access. What struck me first was that I couldn't believe that I'd walked up and down to the lower valley base of Saas Grund, where I'd spent the summer under canvas at the campsite on my previous trip. It looks (and is) unbelievably steep and hard work, even in a van! I guess when you're younger and on a tight budget (and don't know any better), that's just what you get on and do!

Back then, having ridden the train from Geneva Airport and arrived in the village on the yellow Post Bus, my main memory was the mind-blowing scenery and equally out of this world shop prices. Tired, hungry, and laden down with camping and climbing kit, we had tried to find somewhere to eat and sleep. I remember the price of a takeaway burger being about half our weekly budget and then receiving the news from the tourist office that the campsite was in fact way down below us in the lower valley. It was an inauspicious start to my alpine climbing career, as too tired to lug all the gear down to the campsite, my climbing partner and I were forced to bivi in the woods just off the side of the path as it got dark. As we bedded down on the flattest bit of ground we could find, we laughed at the plus side to this which was a saving in campsite fees. It would at least lessen the blow of our first shopping experience.

This time, by making use of the Mittelallin Lifts, we were transported from a cold car park in Saas-Fee, to a much colder top ski-lift station at around 3500m. This left us with just over 500m of vertical height gain to reach the summit of a 4000m peak. If only it were that simple though! While the angle of the approach was gentle enough, the surrounding glacial terrain gave a menacing feel. Strong winds had stripped away most of the fresh snow and we needed our ski crampons to gain some purchase on the hard icy surface. Without them, a large degree of control is lost as the skis slip and slide, not helpful or ideal when it's imperative to stay on a certain track. We'd dealt with this kind of thing before, so initially, it was no major concern. What soon became a major concern though was the proximity of the enormous, wide, gaping crevasses that the route passed through. Although roped together, it was still a tense time, as we shuffled past the slots that disappeared out of sight into bottomless dark green and blue voids. Our pace slowed as we made sure that each ski was firmly gripped to the surface before committing our weight to it.

Crevasses are the cracks that open on the surface of the glacier as a result of its imperceivably slow, gravity-assisted journey downhill. The solid mass of accumulated snow and ice can't always bend or distort with the movement, so cracks appear over time. During the winter months, they are often filled with snow creating snow bridges that allow mountaineers safe passage. But on this occasion, the crevasses seemed to be everywhere, wide open, and far too close for comfort.

By the time we reached the Feejoch at just over 3800m, the combined effect of cold, wind, ice and terrifying terrain, all came together to help us decide to call it a day. We were supposed to be enjoying ourselves, not getting scared out of our minds! On the safer terrain of the col, away from the maze of crevasses, we were able to take in the incredible views and have a breather and a bite to eat. At least this time around, I was able to take in the panorama with more clarity.

With composure regained, we prepared for an equally cautious return leg back to the sanctuary of the ski station. Here, we both heaved a huge sigh of relief as we dropped onto the safety of the immaculately groomed pistes of the patrolled ski area. The cold wind remained for the day, but the disappointment of not making the summit was made up for with a fine day enjoying the ski runs and with the ease of the lifts. A few thousand meters of ascent and descent later and only once we'd wrung every last Swiss Franc out of our ski passes, we clunked across the car park in our ski boots and collapsed into the van.

Travelling and living in the back of a small van, requires discipline and systems. As in our case, if there are two of you, there needs to be a willingness to share an above-average amount of personal space. Everything needs to have a place or there is not enough room for everything to fit and it's surprisingly easy to lose things in such a small area. The dimensions of an Escort Van are certainly modest when compared to the average campervan, but perfectly functional when that's all the space you have available. Unlike a campervan, access is via the two back doors as there are no side doors, other than for the driver and passenger. The internal length is exactly that of my height and was a critical factor when deciding on what model to purchase. This means that when in 'sleep mode' there is enough space for us both to lie down albeit in a slightly friendly way. On the right-hand side, my Dad had constructed a wooden storage chest, which did impede the already limited sleeping space, but the benefits of a storage area, bench seat and cooking table outweighed that of having enough space to toss and turn.

Carefully, we de-kitted ourselves from ski mode and climbed into our mobile living space. At least the cold conditions meant that the snow brushed easily from our clothes and skis, leaving us with no wet kit to deal with. There was a mix of emotions on arriving back. A satisfying glow of exhilaration from the skiing was mixed with the relief of being out of crevasse danger and back into the safe cocoon of the van. Our minds and bodies could now start to come down from high alert as we relaxed into the life-giving warmth of a hot drink. Out of our stiff ski boots, our toes were flexed and massaged with warm fingers. Feeling our muscles relax, our shoulders dropped without the burden of rucksacks or high stakes decision making. There was no major rush to depart and after our early start, the decision to stay over was an easy one. We'd also made a loose arrangement to try and meet up with our friends Pete and Dave (whose van we were parked next to), which gave another good reason not to rush away. We managed to get one more brew on and some food in us before darkness and the overwhelming fatigue arrived. Then we were more than happy to nestle into the comfort of our down sleeping bag nest.

Verbier, Switzerland
Tourist Information Area Layby Under the "Welcome to Verbier" Sign

April 20th 2005

LOGBOOK ENTRY:
"En route from Chamonix to Verbier. A fine camping spot down by the river. Weather looking like we might even get some sun tomorrow".

During our time in Switzerland, we would often nip over the border into France to visit a friend who lived in Chamonix. His well-placed apartment in the centre of town would always have several climbers lodging there, but somehow, space was usually found for a couple more within the confines of the magical Tardis. We had met Stu the previous year and formed a friendship through climbing and over a memorable Christmas ice-climbing trip to Rjukan in Norway. In pursuit of gaining his Mountain Guide qualification, he had bought what became known as the 'Cham-Pad', a property which soon became the second home to many transient and aspiring alpinists.

Situated directly under Mt Blanc, on the French side of the mountain, Chamonix has become a bustling hub for mountaineers and for good reason. You can't help but walk around with your neck craning up at the wild skyline and the glaciers that adorn the hillsides seem almost close enough to touch. Yet amongst all this rugged scenery, the town of Chamonix provides all the trappings of modern city life: pubs, clubs, fine foods, and expensive shops. For many, it's a place to see and be seen, with an eclectic mix of residents, visitors, sightseers and skiers. Along the busy high street, you'll be brushing shoulders with the immaculately dressed, ultra-wealthy on their way to the Prada boutique, as well as ski bums living on a shoestring. You'll see people heroically celebrating their first alpine forays in packed bars alongside experienced alpinists who have just returned from climbing some of the hardest and most committing alpine routes in the world.

In many other sports, the elite players or athletes are only ever seen from a distance - on a magazine cover, or television coverage, but in the outdoor world, and particularly in Chamonix, you can bump into total legends while buying a baguette or ordering a beer. Frequently, there'd be someone I'd just read about in a mountaineering magazine crashed out among a pile of battered climbing gear at the Cham-Pad, having just returned from a few days spent lashed to a particularly steep and scary north face. Over a cup of weak Lipton 'Yellow Label' tea, they'd modestly explain what they just climbed as if it were no big deal, complete with particular bits of beta in case I was thinking of repeating the route any time soon. It's a heady mix. A miniature alpine city – the bustle of London, but with better scenery, more mountain interest and all packed into the confines of a steep-sided valley. It felt like another world compared to the sleepy little Swiss village that we lived in.

All of this comes with a price of course, along with the cost of accommodation, a ski pass to the Chamonix valley is one of the most expensive ones you can purchase in the whole of the Alps.

I'd skied here a couple of times during the winters while at university but luckily the cost of living was reduced considerably, thanks to my friend Daragh who knew of a shack in the woods above the town that was free for climbers or skiers to live in. It was the kind of place where an induction or introduction was required and while many people that we met had heard of the infamous 'Le Shack', very few had been there or knew of its precise location. It was a closely guarded secret and back then our admission came with the caveat that we were not to reveal its location, to preserve the air of mystery as well as to keep it from becoming overpopulated. The inhabitants of the Shack varied over time, but Daragh had lived there previously so we were greeted with open arms. As is often the way in the outdoor world, as well as Daragh knowing one of the shack dwellers from a previous stay, we had several friends in common which seemed to further endorse our membership to the limited, and as we were to find out, sought after space.

It was a chalet in miniature. Wooden carvings adorned the exterior walls of the building and the entrance was through a tiny but sturdy door, about a metre high and which hung on large metal hinges. With only one small window, once inside, it always took a few moments for your eyes to adjust to the light. A bench that was just about long enough to stretch out on was the full width of the building. Posters, stickers and flags hung from the walls and there were layers of graffiti and initials that had been etched in the wood of the ceiling over the years. At the side of the wooden building, outside the tiny window, was an old bicycle which was bolted to the floor and hooked up to a car battery. In the mornings, a short peddle would be sufficient to light a small lamp and bring the radio crackling into life.

The facilities were basic but functional; hygiene levels were questionable. A small sink with a single tap drew water from the spring outside and during the coldest nights had to be left running to prevent it from freezing. In the corner, a stove fashioned from an old oil drum provided the heat next to a double-ring gas burner. A loft hatch led up to a sleeping platform that could sleep five at a push. One year finding the platform full, we took up temporary residence on the two benches below. The general rule seemed to be that each evening everyone would return with some food products, which between us could be fashioned into some sort of meal. It was a happy, friendly and economic way to experience the skiing and climbing of the Chamonix valley, as long as you were okay with scrimping on hygiene for a few days.

This time I was happy to just come to Chamonix for the social, a change of scene and a bit of window shopping, before heading away to find a new area to ski that was both less crowded and cheaper to access.

We drove over the Col du Montets and back into Switzerland to the ski resort of Verbier. Although not exactly a cheaper alternative, we'd heard so much about the place during the winter that we felt that we couldn't let the season finish without skiing some of their infamous slopes. As it turned out, having spent a stormy day loitering around the unaffordable shops in Chamonix, the weather did improve for our day on skis around Verbier. While Mt Fort and the ski area had been shrouded in mist for a few days, the breaks in the cloud revealed a good covering of fresh snow ready for us to spend the next day putting new tracks in.

Sun was flooding into the back of the van as we happily cooked up by the river, feeling the warmth and that Verbier really was 'Welcoming Us' as the road sign had declared. Well-fed, watered and rested, we were up in time to be on the first lift, where we milked the ski pass for all it was worth. Only once the chairlifts had stopped turning and our legs couldn't take any more bulldozing through fresh snow, did we return to the van and head for home feeling utterly and happily exhausted.

Grindelwald, Switzerland
Just below the North Wall of the Eiger

April 25th 2005

LOGBOOK ENTRY:
"Have joined the fleet of other campervans who are blatantly ignoring the 'No Overnight Parking' signs. Beautiful views - and tomorrow a walk under the famous north face".

Heading off the beaten track in search of less well known and more importantly, less frequented places is our usual preference. With a wealth of knowledgeable and experienced friends in the village where we lived, we were given no shortage of itinerary suggestions, but we couldn't spend a year in Switzerland and not go and see the North Face of the Eiger, even if it was a tourist hotspot. Outside of the French-speaking Canton where we lived, I was as surprised as Clare was to discover that I could actually speak a bit of German and understand some of the signs in this Swiss-German speaking area of the country. Words seemed to pop out of my mouth before I even had the chance to think about a reply, thanks to a GCSE in German and a school exchange trip. Who knew that I'd been hoarding all that knowledge from years ago?

Grindlewald and its celebrity mountain were every bit as impressive as I'd read and heard, so it was no surprise that there were plenty of other people in town to check out the views, even during the 'off-season'. It was clear that the train from the village to the summit station was way out of our budget, but we were happy to take in the view from the valley and although I had no intention of setting foot on the face, I was interested to see where the historic lines of ascent went. Along with the Matterhorn, the Eiger is undoubtedly one of Switzerland's 'flagship' peaks and a key part of any tourist's itinerary as well as a serious lure to any alpinist.

The night in the van had been relatively uneventful and despite the array of notices that ordinarily would have moved us along to somewhere more discrete, there was a general feeling of safety in numbers in the layby. To be fair, it was a good place to park for the night and it seemed unlikely that we would all get moved on, so we slept peacefully packed in amongst our rucksacks and winter kit.

The following day was made a success thanks to the friendly advice that we'd been given from friends back home in Villars. Advice, which was much more reliable than the previous month, when we'd been encouraged to make a ski journey off the Diablerets glacier, where we'd been told we would be 'well away from the crowds' – a journey that was nearly the end of us.

I will digress from our wonderfully pleasant and well-planned Eiger excursion to share the story of the less well-planned adventure on the Diablerets glacier. Although not started or finished with a van bivi, it shows the stark contrast between doing your research properly rather than taking advice at face value!

There is a very fine multi-day ski touring journey from the summit of Diablerets across several spectacular peaks, but we'd been told that it was possible to do a single long day journey that could be finished with a run down to the valley or by taking a small cable car into a neighbouring valley. From there the bus could be taken back up the road to the col where the ski lifts start. The general premise sounded great.

The route description that I'd been given was, admittedly a little vague, but it seemed to tie up with the map, so we decided to give it a go. Buses didn't seem to be that regular, but I was fairly confident that we'd be able to thumb a lift back up to the ski station once we reached the road.

Things started on the familiar terrain of the ski area that we'd been visiting since the lifts first opened for the season but skiing down past the base of the last lift and out of sight of any human interference felt a little spooky. Beyond the confines of the ski area, there was not a sound to be heard except for the swish from our skis and the panting of our breath as we picked the best line of descent. A small skin up a minor summit gave enough of a view to navigate our way down to the cable car that was marked on our map as well as somewhere to stop for a rest.

As we sat having some food, we noticed another small team skiing on the other side of the valley, which gave us a little encouragement that someone else had also chosen to head this way, as up to now, we'd seen no signs of life – not even an old ski track. It certainly wasn't a well-travelled itinerary.

The terrain and situation continued to have a wild feel about them and we both had a nervous sense of uncertainty as we continued our descent.

This was compounded some more when the 'cable car' came into view. We could see the cable, but there were no cars. It just didn't feel 'right'.

The other team reappeared into view as we neared the top of the lift, which was not representative of the busy ski hub that I had been envisaging. Instead of finding a kiosk, bar and deckchairs in the snow, there was just a small, plain, deserted cabin, where the cable ended. Instead of the sound of music, the chinking of drinks and the chatter of skiers, there was silence. Something was seriously amiss.

With nowhere else to go and with a sinking feeling in our bellies, we travelled over to the cabin to see if the other skiers knew something that we didn't. They spoke in German, which was completely lost on us, before bringing things down to my GCSE language level, then doing their best in English to relay some alarmingly disappointing information. It turned out that the cable car was some sort of service line and had nothing to do with skiing or skiers. More bad news came in receiving the next bit of local knowledge - it was possible to ski down to the valley below, but it was a difficult ski and exposed to avalanches. This was very bad news indeed as we were now far from home, far from help and without enough time (or energy) to retrace our steps back to our starting point. Neither of us was equipped or willing for a night out in the open.

That's when it occurred to us to ask what the other skiers planned to do. Luckily for us, they did have a plan, having sourced much better information than us before setting out. They had arranged and paid for someone to open the cable car and come up with a private cabin to take them down to the valley. They seemed pretty unimpressed about sharing, especially when the cabin arrived and it was clearly going to be a squeeze with just them in it. However, they took pity on us and much to our relief, we were allowed to wedge into the tiny metal box and were given safe passage down to the safety of the valley.

As the cramped box descended, the line of the ski descent became clearer and I was left with a slightly sickly feeling. It would have been impossible to have read the route from above and weaving around through some enormous cliffs would have been terrifying at best. We thanked our lucky stars and determined to get better information before ever setting out on skis again. Having prised ourselves out of the cabin and onto the tarmac, we found ourselves at a small car park in a forest. The offer of some Swiss Francs was declined, but a lift was still given, in their waiting car, back up the valley to be reunited with the van.

Returning to the story of visiting the Eiger North Wall, you may be pleased to hear that we learnt from the drama of the ill-fated Diablerets experience. This time, armed with a map, guidebook and an itinerary that had been checked and double-checked, we enjoyed a very enjoyable excursion.

Interlaken, Switzerland
In the forest on the edge of town

April 26th 2005

LOGBOOK ENTRY:
"After a fine day out in the snow, under the North Face of the Eiger, we returned to Interlaken in search of a van bivi site. Found the perfect spot by the lakeshore, but it was well signed with 'Camping Verboten' boards, so had to move on once it got dark.
Have ended up on the edge of a large forest area at the start of a Par Course Vita trail. Maybe we'll be doing some pull-ups and jogging in the morning...?"

To keep a low profile on our van excursions, a tactic that would sometimes be employed was to find somewhere beautiful to spend the evening, where we could cook up dinner and enjoy the sunset, before driving on to a more discreet but less picturesque place to sleep. Because the van was so small and adaptable, it meant that it was relatively easy to move on without a major re-sort in the back. This was a case example, where evening dining and lakeside appreciation could be fully and legitimately taken part in, but a sounder sleep was always much more likely when there's not a sign outside saying no overnight parking or camping!

The 'North Wall' might get all the attention, but nearby there are also other cliffs of a much more friendly nature. For those less inclined to take on the additional hazards of avalanche, rockfall and verglas, there are some spectacular, if less historic, bolted routes nearby. These fitted our criteria much better, so having had our day of ogling upwards in the shadow of the mighty celebrity, we set our attention on some just as steep, but much less committing multi-pitch climbing.

Zinal, Switzerland
At the end of the road

May 4th 2005

LOGBOOK ENTRY:
"After an attempt on reaching the Weisshorn Hotel on skis, we were defeated by waist-deep sugary snow and forced to retreat to lower altitudes. Drove along the valley to the deserted town of Zinal. Found a lovely spot at the end of the valley, next to the river (good flower identification terrain). We're just outside of the car park that says 'No Overnight Parking', so somehow that seems to make our presence okay. A cold night, since it started to snow. Didn't bode well for the next day, but hot chocolates and down sleeping bags have made it yet another enjoyable van bivi".

During our year in Switzerland, I had been working hard to gain my International Mountain Leaders Award (IML). I had already been trained and assessed to lead groups in the United Kingdom by gaining both the summer and winter Mountain Leaders Awards and the newly created IML was the next logical step. A broad depth of experience built over many seasons and years is required before you are allowed to put yourself forward for training or assessment as a mountaineering professional. The reason for this is that mountain experience cannot be taught through a single course or handbook. In the ever-changing outdoor environment, the safe or most efficient thing to do in a given situation will change and develop depending on a whole host of factors. The list of variables is almost unending, but even just considering the basic elements, such as what the weather is like, the temperature or available equipment, will lead to a myriad of options. Having first-hand experience with different conditions helps the experienced mountaineer arrive at the best course of action in each circumstance. And then, of course, there's your group to look after!

Without strict right or wrong answers, passing the rigorous assessment process can only be achieved by having lived through all types of mountain conditions and having learnt about the pros and cons of each on quality mountain days. These days out, which also need to be in a variety of different mountain ranges and seasons, all need to be carefully amassed and recorded in the infamous 'Mountain Leader Logbook' to verify your claims. Naturally, these days it's in an online digital logbook, but the information and relevant details remain the same. A candidate can put themselves forward for the assessment test when they deem themselves to be ready and their log is scrutinised by the assessors before the test begins. Having now been on the other end of this process as a trainer and assessor, it's an invaluable and telling resource and no surprise that those with an extensive breadth of experience and days out in the mountains are almost always the strongest candidates during the assessment week compared to those who have just managed to log the minimum requirements. Experienced mountaineers can then be taught how to be good leaders of a group because the other complexities of route finding, weather watching and so on are already second nature to them.

As well as ensuring that you can get a group of clients safely up and back again from any given summit or mountainous region, there are also other considerations aside from navigation and leadership theory. One of which is the necessity to have a broad range of environmental knowledge. Having already earnt a Degree in Outdoor and Environmental Education, I was well ahead of the pre-requisites in terms of knowledge of mountain formations, geography, geology and so on, but when it came down to the smaller scale things such as fauna and flora, I still had a lot to learn.

With a grandfather who earnt his living as a horticulturist and having been brought up by parents who would instinctively point out different flowers and trees, I was slightly disappointed that I'd not retained more of this information over the years. For some reason, I'd either not listened, simply forgotten, or as I prefer to think, that despite storing this information the files had accidentally been removed along with the brain tumour a few years back. Whatever had happened to the knowledge that my parents had tried so hard to instil, it certainly wasn't available on-demand in the way that is considered appropriate for the budding International Mountain Leader. An upgrade was clearly required!

And that is the long story of how Clare and I came to be sitting in the meadows of the Zinal Valley in Switzerland one fine spring morning. Well established amidst the long grass, armed with a borrowed hardback copy of 'Alpine Flowers', we were surrounded by an incredible splash of colourful flora. The mid-altitude meadows of the Alps during spring give a feeling of change and hope, a sign that the alpine summer is returning. They are wonderful places to be and very much recommended for the unrushed.

When the snow has receded, the grass, having spent the last few months cold, wet, and crushed under a meter or so of snow begins to make a comeback. Under the life-giving light of the sun, the yellowing shoots and blades turn a vibrant green and undergo a natural growth spurt. The crocuses are generally the first flowers to bravely make an appearance between the broken patches of slushy melting snow. Purple, yellow and white flames push up to signal that a change in season is afoot. As the grasses rise around them, the race is on for each species to gain a footing and contribute to the colourful hillside decorations.

Slowly, but not particularly methodically, we worked our way around the hillside, diligently stopping to identify what we could, making notes and even taking the odd photo for later testing. This method of learning suited me very well and whenever the opportunity would present itself, we would try and learn a few more species. As with so many things, it was certainly more effective, memorable and fun than simply studying from a book indoors.

Although the flowers were great, the Zinal Valley is also (usually) a great place for late-season skiing on the spring snow, so naturally, we had come prepared to take advantage of this. To the non-skier, it's easy to assume that snow is all the same. The cold white stuff that falls out of the sky each winter turns the Alps into a winter wonderland and the UK roads into a driver's nightmare. But snow is not just snow in the same way that clouds are not just clouds.

The Greenlandic Inuit have hundreds of words to describe snow and given that each snowflake is still thought to be unique, that's no real surprise. If a certain type of cloud can be an indicator of the type of weather that is present, then a certain type of snow can give valuable clues as to how the progress of a mountaineer will fare. Having the experience of being in the mountains over different seasons allows you to experience these different types of snow and know the pros and cons of each. In the Zinal Valley, we got to experience some of the worst types of snow that a ski tourer could find themselves in.

When a snowflake first forms and the delicate lattice of microscopic complexity begins falling from the cloud that created it, it is at the start of a journey of change. Even in laboratory conditions, a snowflake gradually metamorphoses through a process of sublimation. Outdoors on an open mountainside, the changes can happen much quicker and changes in the individual snowflakes will create subsequent changes in the snowpack lying on the ground. Wind, rain, sunshine, and temperature variations will all play their parts in this process and a snowpack that is skied in the morning will often provide a very different experience when skied later in the afternoon.

Towards the end of the ski season, the intricately delicate crystals that fell at the beginning of the winter have melted and combined into a more granular texture. On a spring morning, this 'corn snow' can provide an excellent firm base for skiing. As the sun starts to warm the surface, a satisfying slushy layer can be sprayed from each 'swoosh' of a ski turn. Once the slope has had too much exposure to the morning sun, the satisfying slushy layer that provided so much pleasure earlier, begins to degrade into a wet and heavy snowpack that has the consistency of wet concrete. Trying to ski through a slope made of wet concrete is as difficult as it sounds. Skis sink in too deep and require great effort to be forced into turns, with each one risking damage to the rider's knees. As well as being unpleasant to ski on, if the angle of the slope is steep enough, the chances of an avalanche are greatly increased as the wet snow is no longer held together with sufficient cohesion to resist the pull of gravity.

And that's the exact kind of snow that we found ourselves floundering about in that morning above the small village of St Luc, in the Zinal Valley. Above us, the imposing sight of the Weisshorn Hotel offered a good resting high point, but upward progress was completely thwarted. We were too late in the day. The sun was beating down, melting the snow but roasting us with an energy-sapping effect as we sank deeper and deeper into the wet sugary slush. They say that good judgement comes from experience and experience comes from poor judgement. Now with the benefit of hindsight, I was inclined to agree - it had been a poor route choice given the conditions but a valuable experience, nevertheless. The retreat down to the van was even more tiring than the way up, with each turn needing a conscious calculation of timing and exertion of effort.

The tracks we left behind were all over the place. Long traverses, wide careering turns, interspersed with impact marks from fallen bodies or deep holes where the snow had simply given way under the weight of the passing skier. It was a relief to be back on terra firma in one piece, without having sustained any injuries. The disappointment of not reaching the hotel and the battle in the rotten snow was soon forgotten having made it back to the van. With a short drive down the valley, armed with a blanket, flower guide, food and drink, we made the most of the remaining glorious afternoon soaking up the sun and flower knowledge in the meadows.

Finale Ligure, Italy
Rocca di Perti

May 16th 2005

LOGBOOK ENTRY:
"Gone to Finale in Italy - on the Mediterranean coast! We drove up a road that eventually ended on a dirt track, near the cliffs of Rocca di Perti. Parked up in a gap between the trees so we could get straight up and go climbing in the morning. Unfortunately, Clare is poorly sick and has been up all night coughing".

After spending a long and enjoyable alpine winter on skis, we had begun to transition back into rock climbing mode. Ski touring had made our legs strong, but not done much for our arms, which tired quickly on our first few forays. As the snow began to recede, we made use of the many south-facing, warm crags that littered the vineyards above the Rhone Valley. Often a short drive down the hill from where we lived would give a noticeable temperature rise and we often, optimistically, left home on a dull or damp morning where misty clouds would hug the hillsides to discover the lower valley basking in the sunshine.

The middle mountains at this time of year are not the safest place to be hanging around. As spring arrives, temperatures rise, and the snow begins to thaw. Ice that has spent the winter expanding into cracks and clinging onto rocks begins to loosen its grip. Expansion pressure when the ice formed is enough to shatter rock and once detached from the icy hold of the mountain, a single tumbling rock can knock another and a chain reaction is released, often to dramatic effect. From the safety of the meadows near our chalet, we sat out on the grass a few times in early May waiting and watching for one of nature's shows to unleash itself. Just as with a thunderstorm, the lightning, or in this case the movement of snow, rock or ice, if spotted can be seen seconds before the sound waves hit, bringing a thunderous roar that echoes into the valley. It's a terrifying sound and sight but from a safe enough distance, it is quite an incredible thing to watch as snow pours like waterfalls, freefalling from cliffs and couloirs, leaving a trail of utter destruction in its wake. Tree trunks snapped like twigs give a visual representation of the power of nature and the need to treat it with respect.

Away from the drama of the rockfalls and avalanches, amongst the mellow vineyards of the Rhone Valley, a taste of summer could be had as well as a great place to get into the flow of rock climbing. Having generally easy access and a sunny aspect, the routes are mostly bolted, which means that the ascending climber can protect the climb by clipping bolt hangers, which have been predrilled and placed every few metres when the route was created. Known as 'sport climbing', it gives an extra element of safety compared to traditional climbing, where the leader can protect the climb by finding cracks and fissures to place wire wedges and camming devices (later removed by the seconding climber).

Without having to worry about finding protection and then spending time safely placing it correctly, sport climbs allow you to concentrate on the actual climbing and athletic movement, with less concern should you fall. That said, having learnt to climb on the cliffs and mountains of the United Kingdom, using 'natural protection', the adage that the lead climber should not fall, had been firmly instilled in us. Subsequently, the idea of falling off was not a notion that we were often keen to entertain. Even with the protection of bolts, we generally, tended to err on the side of caution as we got used to trusting this new style of climbing.

Switzerland is a landlocked country and although we had access to some big lakes, it had been ages since we'd seen the distant horizon over the sea. Chatting with my co-worker Andy while packing away some expedition gear, we were, as usual, swapping notes and stories on various climbing areas and making plans for the coming weeks. When I mentioned the sea, Andy began bubbling away excitedly about a place in Italy on the Mediterranean coast that was a mecca for sport climbing. Espresso coffee, pizza, climbing, the sea and of course, glorious sunshine, were all cited as individual reasons alone to go. As soon as our work was done, a map was produced and an itinerary began to take shape.

The next day, Andy appeared with a well-thumbed copy of the local climbing guidebook and we were sold. It's one of the great bonuses of living and working around like-minded folk. Not only can you share the psych and enthusiasm to come up with new adventures, but maps, guidebooks and equipment were all willingly loaned to us.

The timing of our Italian adventure was coinciding nicely with Clare's birthday. And why just have a birth 'day' celebration, when you could have a 'birthday week' – especially when you can spend it in Italy! Having had the route highlighted on our trusty European Road Atlas in bright pink pen, we now had a visual idea of where we were heading. With a combination of snowy roads and non-4x4 transport, our initial concern that we had to cross a high alpine pass was put to rest when we noticed that the Swiss had very kindly dug a tunnel underneath the Grand St Bernard Pass. The only slight snag came when we realised how much it cost to drive through the tunnel, but we were already committed by that time!

At some considerable distance underground inside the longest tunnel that either of us had ever been in, we came across a road blockade of armed guards. It was the Italian border. We were halted and the contents of the van were briefly perused, while our passports were taken away for inspection. It was probably only a few minutes, but it felt like forever and we both spent the wait trying not to look guilty or suspicious. It's hard not to when you're surrounded by machine guns in what could easily pass as a scene from a James Bond film.

With our toll paid, passports were returned along with a 'Grand St Bernard Tunnel' sticker to add to the interior decor. We pulled away slowly, mindful of the speed limit and with eyes flicking nervously to and from the armed officials in the rear-view mirrors. Exiting the tunnel was like arriving in a completely different world – here on the south side of the mountain range, the snow had long since melted and the grassy meadows were full of summer colour. The sunlight was blinding as our eyes took a moment to adjust to the sight of the Aosta Valley laid out below us. A gradual winding motorway took us gently down away from the mountains and into the warm industrial valley below.

Our early start from home meant that we were going to have time to break up the journey with a quick climb at nearby Macherby. We had no guidebook for this crag but had it marked on our map by Andy, who had insisted that we stop there. Outside of the UK, it's not uncommon to find the name of the climb painted on the rock at the base of the route. It's a rather handy way of identifying that you are indeed about to get involved with the correct climb, but something that would be considered utter vandalism in the British mountains.

Here at Macherby, this was taken another step further as we discovered the name, length and difficulty of the climbs were all inscribed on small metal plaques at the base of each route. Just on the edge of the parking area, there was even an overview topo of the whole cliff. We had to marvel at it. And with the base of the (enormous) slabs of rock just a few strides away from the van, this really was roadside climbing like nothing we'd ever seen. The climbs ranged from single pitches to long multi-pitch routes and the bolted belays meant that descent could be made at any point. All in all, it was quite a place – and to think that this was merely a prelude to what we were heading for added to the buzz.

Despite the ease of access and identification, the rock type and style of climbing were totally different to the limestone of the Rhone Valley and everything felt much harder than we were used to. Still, we battled our way up a route or two, then retreated to the van with grazed knuckles and a decent sweat on before continuing south. The main road was easy to follow, but it took us a while before we eventually caught sight of the coast. It was dusk by the time we located our chosen crag, but conveniently, there was a flat, quiet spot in amongst the trees, which looked like the perfect place to let us and the van rest. In the morning, the climbing would be just a stone's throw away...

Finale, Italy
Roadside outside of town

May 17th 2005

LOGBOOK ENTRY:
"Having got halfway up a route, the heavens opened forcing us to make a hasty retreat. So much for Mediterranean climbing. It's not the scene that Andy P had portrayed. Checked out the beach and town instead. Quiet. Despite lots of driving about, found nowhere to stay. Eventually pulled up in a small layby outside Finale just before dark. A huge electrical storm ensued - thunder and heavy, heavy rain, which sounded even louder inside our tin bedroom. I slept on my good ear but could still hear the rain drumming down on the metal roof. Clare was almost driven to distraction by it! Not a good night".

A light mist was blowing around the top of the crag in the morning and the temperatures were a far cry from the image that I'd painted in my mind of the area. Breakfast was a rushed affair as it was clear that rain was on the way. Having come this far we were determined to at least get some climbing in. This time, armed with an actual guidebook, we'd pre-selected where to head before going to sleep, so the approach and location of our chosen climb were relatively straightforward. One pitch in, just high enough to be above the tree line and able to survey our surroundings, the pitter-patter arrived, signalling the end to any further upward progress.

From our vantage point, you didn't need to be a weather forecaster to predict that this was going to be more than just a passing shower. Climbing in the rain, especially on this kind of rock type wasn't just going to be unpleasant, it was going to be dangerous, bordering on impossible. As the light grey of the limestone turned dark with the impact of each raindrop, the friction upon which we relied was quickly all but lost. Frustrating, but with an easy abseil back to the ground, it meant that we were in the shelter of the van before long and pondering our next move.

Before leaving home, we had pictured ourselves climbing pitch after pitch of gloriously warm, sun-kissed rock, ticking off the classic routes of the area. Then as the sun started to dip, in the late afternoon, after a celebratory cappuccino in the shade of the town square café, we'd cool off with a refreshing swim in the crystal-clear waters of the Mediterranean. Diving down deep between shoals of multi-coloured fish, we'd float weightlessly while the chalk and sweat from our hands and bodies were washed clean by the refreshing salty water. With our hair drying in crusty curls, we'd soak up the final warmth from the last colourful rays of sunshine as the clouds on the horizon turned pink to red. Parked up by the sea wall, looking out at the distant horizon, we'd cook in the back of the van, feeding our tired bodies with a healthy and nutritious meal, before falling into a long, deep and satisfying sleep.

But sometimes, things just don't quite work out as planned and not for the first time, the image in my mind turned out to be very starkly different to what we encountered. It's good to have plans, but with most outdoor activities, it's also important to make sure that the plan is flexible. We can control a lot of things and stack the odds in our favour, but when it comes to the weather, we had to take what we were given and make the most of it. These days, of course, it's very easy to check a multitude of different weather forecasting models and detailed predictions and even check a webcam in real-time from your phone, but back then, the passing of information was of a much slower speed, so you could either wait for the perfect conditions, or you could just get out there and give things a go. We usually opted for the latter and more often than not, we'd get away with getting something done, but after the long drive south, on this occasion, we had to make do with our single pitch of climbing on dry rock before admitting defeat.

As predicted from the belay ledge, a passing shower it was not. Several cups of tea later, we finally accepted the fact that things were not going to be drying out any time soon and as comfy as the van was, neither of us was keen to spend a whole day festering in the back. As we drove along the coast to get a new view, the intensity of the rain and later accompanying wind, grew and grew. Optimistically, we checked out a few other crags as a reconnaissance for future visits but were forced to admit that it wasn't going to be the climbing trip we had envisaged. In summer, the coastline is a busy tourist hotspot, but in pre-season, it was a ghost town and one without any useful van bivi sites or much in the way of shelter for two washed-out climbers. We decided to hang around and see what the morning would bring us, eventually bedding down in a layby on the edge of town. The thunder, lightning and hammering rain on the roof of the van almost drove us stir-crazy!

Gran Paradiso, Italy
Illiaz Campsite

May 18th 2005

LOGBOOK ENTRY:
"Climbed straight into the driver's seat and drove this morning! - It's still raining!! Halfway back to Switzerland, we stopped at Macherby to climb, then headed over to the Gran Paradiso National Park, for the sole reason that we could see some blue sky in that direction! Found (eventually), an actual campsite in Illiaz in the Gran Paradiso National Park. It's dry! Hoorah! Cooked in the van but put up the tent to celebrate the good weather and make the most of our pitch. Happy Birthday for tomorrow, Clare. Gonna go for a climb and have pizza and espresso".

Salvation came not in the form of weather forecasts (remember this was back before smartphones and apps were even a thing), but in the sighting of some blue sky. The journey back north was made without hesitation as there was nothing to be gained by spending another day cooped up in the rain. Back at the crag of Macherby, the skies remained overcast and wet streaks on the rock limited our choice, but we were able to climb a bit. The dusty floor from a day ago was now muddy and the vibe felt very different. A retreat back home seemed inevitable, until a slight brightening in the distant sky changed our minds.

Looking at the map, the clearing in the weather seemed to be located over in the direction of the Gran Paradiso National Park. Neither of us had ever been there, so it seemed like a good enough reason to try our luck just one more time. And having paid to come through the tunnel to Italy, we both felt the need to get our money's worth! With little more than a glimpse of blue sky to aim for, we took the next exit from the motorway and headed west.

We always kept a selection of guidebooks and maps in 'The Library' – an area near the back right-hand door of the van. While we had no climbing guide, we did have a hiking map that covered a small section of the Grand Paradiso. Being a mountainous National Park, we figured that there had to be some climbing somewhere. Given our recent discovery of the convenience of having route names and grades printed at the base of the climbs, we guessed that if we could locate a suitable looking cliff, there was a good chance that we'd find something to climb. We aimed for a likely looking village called Illiaz, which turned out to be a fine bet. Not only was the picturesque hamlet dry and sunny, but it also turned out to be home to plenty of great rock climbing and littered with beautiful waterfalls and plunge pools. In the winter it's transformed into one of the best ice climbing areas in Italy and we later realised that we'd inadvertently turned up somewhere that was already on my list of places to visit – just in a different season!

Our moods changed instantly. A campsite, although practically empty, was open and the 'Birthday Trip' was back on! In a splurge of indulgence to cheer ourselves up, pizza was ordered, and we sampled a genuine 'cappuccino' while the campsite owner pointed out the various crags and climbs in the area.

I can only assume that any Italian who has ever ordered a cappuccino in the UK must be either outraged, disappointed, or bewildered at what is served up under the pretence of being the classic Italian beverage. The drink that I received bore no resemblance to what I had previously only ever encountered outside of the country. It was produced at rapid speed, with the smooth and efficient flair that comes from years of experience. A pull of coffee from the gleaming silver machine, topped with a dash of warm foamed milk made it only just bigger than an espresso, but the silky-smooth liquid tasted incredible. I only wished I could make it last longer. Best of all was that the bill seemed like a giveaway after nearly a year of living with Swiss price tags.

A very happy few days ensued while we made the best of our van camping location. The reasonably priced pitch meant that we could use our tent as the sleeping area and the back of the van could be used as a living and cooking zone creating a much-improved level of comfort. Plus there was the luxury of shower facilities at hand. Some exploratory hikes with marmots and a birthday climb on a beautiful slab of rock above a shimmering turquoise plunge pool topped off the trip, leaving us keen to return one day. What a discovery!

Chamonix, France
(Not technically a van bivi, but a splendid one never-the-less)

May 27th 2005

LOGBOOK ENTRY:
"Left the van near the Col du Montets and climbed the Aiguillette d'Argentine in the Aiguille Rouge near Chamonix. Biving underneath it on a big flat rock looking right out to Mt Blanc and Les Dru on the other side of the valley. Many Ibex came and nestled down around us!"

With the skis packed away and the season officially declared over we turned our attention once again to getting back on the rock. While our legs were as strong as they'd ever been, our arms still needed some work to get up to speed. Generally, our days that spring would be spent in the nearby crags above the vineyards that line the sunny aspects of the Rhone Valley, but whenever we could, we would seek an adventure further afield.

When it came to rock climbing knowledge, apart from our local friends, we had two good guidebooks containing information on all the best rock climbing in the area and were determined to tick off as many of the listed routes as we could. Local climbing legends, the 'Remy Brothers' had produced the definitive guide to the area, with all cliffs and all grades painstakingly documented along with hand-drawn diagrams and maps. We did a good job of working our way through this, gaining a huge knowledge of the region in the process and soon knew which crags were best for the conditions of the day. Morning sun, afternoon sun, slabby routes, steep ones, rock types and cliff heights all played a part in making the best selections. At each crag, we'd climb as many of the best looking or classic routes at our chosen grade as daylight and finger strength would allow.

There was always more to go at, but athletic ability meant that the harder routes were not going to get a look in from us without a serious and dedicated training routine – something that was of limited interest to both of us! One of the great aspects of rock climbing is that anyone, no matter what level of ability, can get the same buzz of excitement and feeling of satisfaction from challenging themself on the rock at a level they want. The same glow of satisfaction can be achieved by someone who completes a technically difficult climb alongside a less experienced or able climber on an easier route. Because the feeling is internal, and we can set the level of difficulty or risk to one that feels most acceptable, no two ascents are the same.

While rock climbing is often glamorised or portrayed in the media as the pursuit of an adrenaline junkie, more often than not, the long and time-consuming nature of ascending a cliff means that the release of chemicals to the brain is a long and drawn-out process that requires a steady head to be kept, rather than receiving the euphoria of a sudden buzz. Having the presence of mind to stay in the zone and focused on the task at hand can provide an almost meditative state. Having the ability to concentrate without distraction, especially in a situation where mistakes can have serious consequences is a fundamental part of rock climbing and for me, certainly one of the attractions.

Down on the ground, there are so many other thoughts that vie for attention and space in my already cluttered mind. But as height and, or difficulty increase, the clutter is soon sifted through and ordered, allowing only the relevant snippets of information to be processed without interference. While there's a lot to know and think about when it comes to climbing, in some ways, it can be a way of reducing the noise.

The pages of our second book, called Plaisir West, document all the best low to medium grade long routes in the western area of the Alps and by now were known almost by heart. Every well-thumbed page provided mouth-watering photographs of climbers in outrageous situations, yet with the tantalizing knowledge that almost every route was within our grade range. On the battered orange cover, the silhouette of a rock climber balanced on top of a lone spire of rock provided the inspiration that led us to bivi high above the valley in the Aiguille Rouge of the Mt Blanc range. The tip of the pinnacle was only just large enough to accommodate both feet of the unknown climber and behind them, the backdrop of shining white mountains was the same as we were now looking out at. For a long time, the page with the topo had been folded over and marked ready on the 'must-climb' list. Now we were finally making an ascent.

The hike up to the climbing at Les Cheresys is without shortcuts but being part of the famous Tour du Mt Blanc long distance trekking route, the trail is well marked and easy to follow. As with many footpaths in the alpine regions, where difficult sections of terrain were encountered, a handy section of ladders had been bolted onto the rocks to assist us. We'd left it until quite late in the day to begin our walk-in as the cool of the evening appealed much more than the scorching sun of the mid-afternoon. As we'd hoped, the only other climbers and hikers we came across were making their way down the path as we were heading up.

With the weather being warm and settled, we'd gone as lightweight as possible for a night out, but with the added rock climbing gear, our packs felt pretty heavy. The consolation was that for the effort of a bit of hard work getting there, we'd hopefully have the pinnacle (known as the Aiguillette d'Argentine) to ourselves, a fine night out under the alpine stars and be in the right place to enjoy climbing the bigger routes on the cliffs behind the following day. Even having left the comfort of the van in a roadside layby below, we were well stocked and well prepared for a good adventure.

Having spent so long, looking at the guidebook photos over the last year, there was great excitement when the pinnacle came into view at last. Happily, we dumped our bags and set about looking at the different routes up it. With no one around, we had the time to relax, cool off and prepare ourselves. Given the amount of erosion around the base and the iconic photo opportunity, it was clear that this was usually a much busier place during peak season.

The other indication of the route's popularity was how polished most of the hand and footholds had become. Rather than the usual rough crystalline granite that the Chamonix valley is famous for when we set off from the dusty ground, we found ourselves gingerly pressing down on smooth edges that had been worn down by the passage of hundreds, probably thousands of ascensionists. Despite the climb being well within our level of difficulty, upward progress still demanded a good level of concentration. Once Clare had reached the summit perch, to replicate the classic photo, I had to leave her tied off and dashed across the hillside to get the angle of the guidebook photo before returning to join her. There is just room for two people to cosy up on the summit, with legs dangling over the edge below us. We sat there for ages, watching the sunset across the Mt Blanc range, only abseiling down once the alpenglow started to fade from the snowy backdrop and the first evening stars were making themselves known.

An almost flat granite slab near the base of the tower was just the right size for two climbers to lay out their sleeping bags. Now that the sun had gone, we got straight inside them to conserve heat and cooked up dinner and drinks on the tiny gas stove. It was only during the last of the light that it occurred to us that perhaps the local Ibex also found this rocky lookout to be a preferred place to spend the night. We were suddenly surrounded! They all had huge horns and looked strong, muscular and not a little put out at our presence, but very kindly nestled themselves in among the boulders around us rather than insisting that we move on through any show of force. Once we got used to them being around, we relaxed again and drifted off while counting shooting stars.

Chamonix, France
Col du Montets

May 28th 2005

LOGBOOK ENTRY:
"Climbed at Les Cheresrys, then bivied at the Col. Nice big layby. Stunner views. Climbing at Vallorcine tomorrow..."

The Ibex had mostly moved on before we showed any sign of vacating the plinth of granite where we'd spent a very comfortable night. At home, I'm not really much of a breakfast in bed kind of guy, but on an open mountainside, in the fresh cool of a bright summer's morning, I was more than happy to be sat up in my sleeping bag taking in the view with a warm mug of tea. The silence of the morning was eventually broken by the sound of the first team of hikers making their way, unseen, above us on the trail. This prompted some movement and slightly reluctantly, we packed away our sleeping kit and stashed it out of sight, before carrying our climbing kit over to the base of the main cliffs.

There are loads of great routes at Les Cheresrys, but the stiff walk up probably prevents a lot of people from bothering to check them out. We were determined to climb as many as possible while we were up there! Feeling accomplished but frazzled by the sun, dehydrated and dusty, we arrived back at the Col at dusk, where for once, we were happy to be sitting in the shade. A candlelight dinner in the back of the van gave us a comfortable and relaxing finish to a great couple of days.

It's in situations like this that we were always grateful to have the van. Being able to fling open the back doors and enter a little haven of comfort always made for a fine end to a day. Always stocked with food and water it was a great mobile base camp. Although far from luxurious, it was our space, where basic comforts could be met and the world shut out if required. It was full of simple pleasures.

Switzerland lay only a short distance away on the other side of the col and in the morning, we rolled down the hill, past the passport border control booth and did a couple of climbs at Vallorcine on the way home.

Chateau D'Oex, Switzerland
Layby just outside of town

June 13th 2005

LOGBOOK ENTRY:
"Expedition reconnaissance. Just paddled a great river with Tom et al. Torrential rain now and massive thunderstorms. We are now sheltering in the back of the van, cooking copious amounts of pancakes and drinking red wine. Can it possibly rain any harder? Concerned that the roof will be dented!"

Determined to make the most of all the opportunities that I was presented with while living in the Alps, I assisted with guiding and coaching a few white-water kayaking groups whenever I could. It was good to keep the skills up as well as sample some of the different types of European rivers. The closest place to kayak was the mighty Rhone which is a milky grey-blue water that flows cold and fast through the plains of the valley base.

Many good afternoons of kayak surfing in the play-wave area were had during my time in Switzerland, but while good fun, surfing a standing wave just doesn't compare to the buzz of reading a river as you journey down it. Having to work out which way to steer the kayak using the power of the water to your advantage provides a very demanding and satisfying experience.

Standing on the bridge near Chateau D'Oex, looking down at the unstoppable rushing flow took me back to my first white water kayaking experience many years before. During my apprenticeship working as a trainee in an Outdoor Education Centre, I was surprised to find that a prolonged period of wet weather had sparked excitement among the other staff. Producing kayaks and other associated bits of equipment from the stores, the rock climbing instructors and mountaineers now switched into kayak mode. I had learnt to kayak during my time in the Scouts, but the local Northamptonshire canal on a windy day had been the most extreme bit of moving water that I had so far encountered. Still, I thought that since I'd passed the first 'star test' of the British Canoe Union, I'd probably be okay on a river and asked if I could join in! Decked out in a long-john wetsuit, some old trainers and other inappropriately basic and borrowed equipment, I enthusiastically joined a team of two to begin the start of my white-water induction.

The recent rains had caused the local river to burst its banks and the drive to the 'get in' now involved a route via partially submerged roads. From the back seat of the overloaded Peugeot, it was difficult in places to determine where the route of the river went. Fields had been turned to lakes of brown standing water and sheep huddled forlornly on hummocks of higher ground. Even to my novice eyes, I nervously suspected that this was going to be a slightly more adventurous day than I had perhaps signed up for. With a car pre-placed at the 'get-out' point, the three of us stood on top of the bridge, while I looked down, somewhat concerned, at the foaming mass of brown water that was charging noisily between the stanchions below us. As the most experienced member of the team, Nick could at least see that he carried a certain duty of care and did his best to describe what he called his 'white-water kayaking 101 crash course'. I tried to point out that I could only see brown water, but he was already in full training mode, bombarding me with new words and terminology that rapidly expanded my vocabulary.

I'd never heard the phrase 'in spate' until then, but Nick assured me that the enormous volume of water would still generally move and behave in the same way as the usual river levels – it was just a question of reading the features. The key to survival on this river, he carried on confidently, would require two things. The first involved the identification of something known as the 'downstream V', which was being demonstrated in real life below me in the form of a smooth tongue of water that was guiding the main flow through the centre of the bridge. As long as I kept hitting the centre of said 'V', I would generally be in the correct place. The second requirement was to make sure that I kept the kayak upright and tried to avoid a capsize at all costs. And with that, the induction was concluded. So, we proceeded to drag our boats upstream to a point in the field where we could access the river.

The water, and seconds later, my kayak were moving at a speed that was hard to process. No sooner was my boat in the flow of the river than I was through the bridge and heading downstream before I had a chance to even consider the whereabouts of any downstream 'V's. Against the odds, with a reasonable sense of balance and in no small part, thanks to a good dose of luck, I made it through the first rapids to where the speed decreased as the energy of the river was absorbed into the wide-open valley. The river had burst its banks and it became apparent that we'd lost the main flow of the river when we found our way blocked by a partially submerged barbed wire fence, indicating we were now kayaking in a flooded field! This is not usually considered part of a river trip. Further rapids, excitement and near misses saw us through the morning with the inevitable parting of boat and paddler coming only a short distance from the end. Dripping on the bank, with paddle still in hand I was fortunate that my borrowed boat was recovered swiftly by my more capable partners. It had been quite a crash course, but one that lay the foundations for many future escapades.

Now, with many years of kayaking experience behind me, the Rhone river in Switzerland provided new interest and challenge. The section of the river at Chateau D'Oex had interesting rapids and a beautiful deep gorge section all adding up to create a great adventure. On this occasion, we were without students, so things were much easier and not just because we didn't get a bus and kayak trailer stuck under a low bridge (but that's another story!).

Kayaking with friends who are equally matched in knowledge and skill on the river means you can rely on each other to make the right call at the right time. Although alone in your boat, teamwork is still essential, with the front kayaker relaying messages about the upcoming rapids and bends via a series of hand signals to help ensure safe passage.

The Chateau D'Oex section provided a suitable level of excitement and we got off the river just in time, as it soon became swollen from the continuing rain. It was nothing like my 'introductory day' back in South Wales, but it was enough to want to be in the safety of dry land again.

While the others headed home due to work commitments, Clare and I were able to stick around for an extra day. Having been gifted a bottle of local wine and with nowhere to go until the next day, we cracked into it while cooking up a pancake feast. With our bags all piled up on the front seats and candles lit, we had a spacious van to entertain ourselves in and enjoy a memorable way to sit out a storm.

As if by design, things had dried up by the morning leaving a pleasant day for hiking a trail to check its suitability for a forthcoming expedition group, which was, I reminded myself, why we had come to Chateau D'Oex in the first place!

Kernow, England
An unremarkable, lone car park

August 6th 2005

LOGBOOK ENTRY:
"House Hunting! Have arrived back from Switzerland and continued to Cornwall..."

The decision to leave our alpine residence, after one year in Switzerland was not an easy one, but Clare had been offered a job in Cornwall, which promised a good change of scene and the chance to brush up on our surfing skills. The term 'alpine residence' perhaps makes our home in the alps sound grander than it was. While it was luxurious compared to a night in the van, it was still basically living in the basement of a large building that was owned by the school. The sizable chalet, which had formerly been built as a fine hotel, had a grand entrance lobby, but our salubrious basement 'apartment' was accessed via a less glamorous tradesman's entrance around the back of the building. While our communal bathroom was a part conversion of the previous 'gent's toilets', complete with old urinals, we did have a private bedroom and a shared living area.

As with most alpine properties, compared to those in the UK, its greatest feature was that it was actually well insulated, so was always warm and dry even during the sub-zero winter temperatures. As an unexpected bonus, our basement area also had a spare room where passing climbers could be quietly housed for a night or two on the sly.

Probably, its best and worst feature was the proximity to the village 'artisan boulangerie'. Each morning the smell of unaffordable fresh bread and pastries would greet us, and our pace would always slow down as we passed by the decorative window display, to ensure that we maximised the sensory stimulation. "One day...", we mused, we'd have to buy something, but we never did. Our limited funds were reserved for ensuring that van diesel took priority over the temptations of the baker's sweet treats.

I had arrived in Switzerland the previous summer, with a modest amount of stuff tossed in the van, just enough to be ready for the ensuing alpine adventures of climbing, skiing and kayaking. As is always the way, over time, an accumulation takes place, and it was a very well loaded van that crossed back over the channel to Dover on the return leg. Thankfully, the customs officers took one look inside the backdoor and while holding back a landside of walking boots and ropes, slammed the door quickly shut again and waved us on our way.

Back on UK soil and after a brief stop to unload some of our belongings at a convenient family base, we continued in a southwest direction in search of some accommodation for the coming year. As it turned out, our assumption that we'd just roll into town and select a suitable dwelling from a long list in the back of the local paper was a touch naïve. Especially during mid-summer in one of the country's busiest tourist counties. Tired, over travelled, and unsure of what the future would hold for us, we eventually chanced upon a quiet and empty car park to spend the night and gather our thoughts.

Talland Bay, Cornwall
Covertly parked outside an unoccupied static caravan

August 7th 2005

LOGBOOK ENTRY:
"Campsites are all full around here, but the site owner has let us park up next to a static caravan that we can pretend to own! Awesome! Slept soundly on the level ground, safe in the knowledge that we would be left undisturbed. Clifftop position, sea view, and a fabulous sunset. Very tired after a day of house hunting (unsuccessful), so nice to have a fine place to chill and sleep."

It was difficult to keep the focus on house hunting on a glorious summer's day when you'd much rather be surfing or climbing. We'd swung past my Auntie Jenny's place to grab a brew to steal us through what turned out to be an exhausting tour of dismal looking properties. Each one was unenthusiastically introduced by an estate agent in an unnaturally shiny suit, sporting too much hair gel. A few other flats that we'd found listed in the local paper and one from a notice board in a local post office also resulted in dead ends for various reasons. It was a deflating start to what should have been an exciting new chapter. We tried not to dwell on the Swiss mountain chalet we had left behind and opted instead to stay hopeful about our new adventure in Cornwall.

The kindness of the campsite owner perked our spirits up and we were able to enjoy the comforts of the van with a big cook-up outside on our makeshift box-lid table. This was followed by a solid sleep, safe in the knowledge that we wouldn't get moved on in the night. A fine van bivi spot can be easily spoilt if there is any uncertainty about the legitimacy of the stay. The threat of police, pranksters or other less-desirables knocking on the door just as you're drifting off to sleep can certainly leave you on edge or ensures only the lightest of restorative sleep is achieved.

As luck would have it, the next day, after a good breakfast taken in the warm morning sun by the back of the van, we got a tip-off about a nearby farm that had a couple of holiday cottages that the owners would potentially be willing to rent to us at the end of the summer season. It turned out to be a perfect stopgap for a few months while we found and purchased a small flat in the coastal town of Torpoint. There was a temporary vibe about living in the holiday cottage, but it did have some advantages, such as a private tennis court and putting green!

Llangollen, Wales
Layby on the A5 between Llangollen and Betws y Coed

September 30th 2005

LOGBOOK ENTRY:
*"Pit-stop en route to an MIA (Mountaineering Instructor Award) workshop, run by the Association of Mountaineering Instructors. Based out of Plas y Brenin - Scrambling in Ogwen and climbing on Bochlwyd Buttress.
Surprisingly spacious with only one person in the back!".*

While the coastline and moors of Cornwall offer a plentiful array of adventurous climbing venues, when it comes to access to the mountains, the choice is limited, to say the least. With only one day of assessment required to finalise the completion of my Mountaineering Instructor Award (now known as the Mountaineering & Climbing Instructor Award), I needed to make a few visits to North Wales over the coming months to be properly prepared. Having managed to pick up a fair amount of local climbing work in Cornwall, I was able to gain a lot of the necessary experience while working under another instructor. This in itself was a stroke of luck, since due to the geography, there were only a couple of qualified MIAs in the whole of the southwest. Despite this climbing work, journeys north were still essential to obtain the necessary mountain experience.

The layby for this van bivi was a definite 'pull in and sleep' type of pit stop. I have spent a few nights there over the years while breaking up the journey, but it wasn't the kind of place to hang around. I'd arrive fed, watered and with a sleeping bag already laid out in the back. Usually, timed well after dark and with my eyes desperate to close and permission to stop concentrating. It was a nice flat place to park for the night and not too affected by the passing traffic. An early departure the following morning would have me in Snowdonia ready and raring to go, with no trace of my passing.

During our time in Cornwall, I'd frequently make this journey to North Wales and to maximise the available climbing time and minimise expenses, I'd leave late on a Friday night and return in time for work on Monday morning. Friday night accommodation would be courtesy of the van and I'd usually be able to find a lounge floor or spare bed at someone's house for the Saturday night. Sometimes I'd climb with friends or fellow trainees, and other times, like this one, I'd take part in a training course or be receiving some mentoring from experienced instructors. They were great weekends and being able to pick the brains of some of the most knowledgeable climbers around was invaluable to my development and ultimately achieving the Mountaineering Instructor Award.

Land's End, Cornwall
Between St Just and Land's End in a little village car park

October 23rd 2005

LOGBOOK ENTRY:
"Awesome day of climbing at Bosigran. Ochre Slab Route II, Severe (4a); Dong, Severe (4b) and Alison Rib, V.Diff. Got rained off Alison Rib so legged it back to the van for a cuppa. Gale force winds and super heavy rains ensued, so cruised into the village. No one was around at the campsite (which just seemed to be the garden of a very scary looking house), so went to the village car park - toilets and all facilities including recycling! Perfect!
After a pasta cook-up inside the back of the van, we dashed to the pub (100m away), but the doorway was blocked by excited Cornish fishermen all weighing their catches! Got soaked while trying to gain their attention. Eventually, they noticed us and welcomed us in. Stayed until we'd dried out, then dashed back to the van."

With new guidebooks to an area that was also pretty new to us, Clare and I would spend the weekends checking out all the best climbing areas that Cornwall and the southwest had to offer. With the addition of wetsuits and surfboards to the quiver of recommended van travelling essentials, we were well prepped for all weather and conditions. If it was dry, we would climb and if it was wet, we would surf. Ideally, the weekend would involve a bit of both activity.

These weekend 'holidays' as we called them took us to all sorts of places and being 'off-season' to the usual tourist busyness, felt like we got to experience a bit of the 'real Cornwall'. Coming across a pub full of enthusiastic, wet, sou'wester-clad fishermen was just one of those experiences and typical of the sort of bonkers situations that the van travels would create for us. Even just a simple overnight trip (and often not even that far from home), would transport us into a whole different world and mindset, with all thoughts of the working week confined to distant memory.

While sometimes we would return home feeling physically exhausted, we always found that we were mentally refreshed. A weekend of van living also had the effect of making our modest little one bed flat feel like the lap of palatial luxury on our return. There's something that makes you really appreciate the simple things when you get back to a real home. Being able just to step into a hot shower or flick a switch and have a kettle boil feels like a delight to be grateful for. And on the flip side of that, away from such comforts, I think that you appreciate the hot drink more if you've had to fill a kettle from a plastic water container, assemble a stove, connect a gas bottle, light it with a hand lighter, then listen for when it starts boiling so you can extinguish the flame before it boils over.

Llangollen, Wales
Northbound Layby on the A5

October 30th 2005

LOGBOOK ENTRY:
"Driving up to Wales (again!) from Cornwall, for more practice for my forthcoming MIA (Mountaineering Instructor Award) test. Between Llangollen and Betws-y-Coed, feeling very tired, I pulled over into the usual layby on the A5. Just climbed in through the back doors. Gave it a good slam and got straight into the awaiting sleeping bag. Head on pillow, just as another car pulls up - A police car!"

I lay very still and very quiet, but a persistent officer comes over and knocks on the back doors. You can't open the back doors from the inside, so I had to perform a contortionist manoeuvre to get to the front door, while inside a sleeping bag (not easy). Pushed open the door and waited for the telling off and being told to move on.

"Having a kip mate?" came the friendly voice behind the torchlight.
"Urrr... Yeah. Feeling a bit too tired to drive on."
"Sorry to have disturbed you then Sir - As you were".

They had seen me climbing into the back of the van and were checking to see that I hadn't been breaking in! Phew! They wished me well on my climbing trip and I went to sleep feeling very safe.

Despite the temporary inconvenience and alarm of having been summoned from the back of the van by a uniformed officer, the resulting sleep was a deep one and well required. A busy work schedule and the knowledge of an impending assessment day had kept my mind and body working hard and I needed to pace myself to make the most of the weekend training raid in North Wales. The following peaceful and uninterrupted sleep was just what I needed and I arrived fully rested, ready for action in the familiar layby of the Ogwen valley where I met my contemporaries the next day.

The to-ing and fro-ing up and down the country finally paid off when the assessment day arrived. Feeling confident and ready, I spent an enjoyable day guiding two clients up and down some of the classic rock climbs at Tremadog, near Porthmadog. I gained safety points early in the day after my assessor, who had gone ahead to rig a safety rope accidentally nearly took out my client. Luckily as soon as we'd arrived at the base of the crags, I'd explained that it would be worth getting our helmets on sooner rather than later, as you never know what might fall from above. No sooner had they buckled their chinstraps tight, but from somewhere up above the assessor fumbled a bit of climbing gear, which dropped the height of the cliff, some 60 metres or so, landing directly on my client's head! Slightly stunned, but otherwise unharmed, he thanked me for my wise and timely advice to don his helmet and we carried on without further incident. By the time we had the ropes out and were ready to climb, the sheepish looking assessor had joined us and assured me that he had no other plans to derail our day or try and wipe any of us out!

There was no time to celebrate with friends in Wales after receiving the congratulatory handshake from the Head of the National Mountaineering centre, as I had to get back on the road to Cornwall. I was probably more relieved than excited to have finally passed, and the journey gave me some good time to soak up the feedback I had received and look back over the journey that had got me there. The award takes years of experience to even be accepted onto the training course, so it was a real milestone to have been one of the few instructors that had made it through to passing the assessment stage. Just like driving a car though, the real learning comes once you're let out on your own, as I'd find out in the years to come. Pumped up from the day's adrenaline, I drove back to Cornwall without a single stop.

Van Life – 2006

Clifftop van bivi at sunset, Cornwall, UK

Ladock, Cornwall
Roadside near the Conybere's

April 29th 2006

LOGBOOK ENTRY:
"Richard and Fiona's 40th Birthday Party - Party in the village hall was cool - pasties aplenty. The Nipper took a tumble on the way home and has sustained minor hand injuries. Somehow, Paulo and I got a go in a Lamborghini! A standard night out in Ladock probably. Van bivied just outside Rich's House - Paulo managed to squeeze a tent in next to us! Splendid sleep - nice flat pitch. Coffee and croissants at Richard's in the morning. Yum Yum. Off to Watergate Bay for a family footie match..."

I have a fair few relatives based in the southwest from my mum's side of the family. With aunties, uncles and cousins dotted around the area, family gatherings were always a pleasure. Richard is one of my cousins, the son of my mum's oldest sister, Janet, who lives in Penzance.

Now that we lived in Cornwall, catching up with this side of the family was much easier. So, when the invite came for Richard and Fiona's 40th party we couldn't wait to join the celebrations.

Even though it was only an hour away it was a fine example of how having a moveable bed for the night just makes things easier. No pre-organising, no tent pitching, no faff and a comfortable place to lie down after a great night of dancing.

Cornwall, England
Cot Valley - End of the road

May 29th 2006

LOGBOOK ENTRY:
"Near St Just - the road goes to a layby just before you drive into the sea. A sign by the van states 'Geological site of national importance - a criminal offence to remove any stones from the beach' - Try telling that to the ocean I thought!"

A day of splendidness and the start of the half-term holidays. After stumbling upon a local music festival last night, we got up and drove west - eventually arriving at Bosigran, to find the world and his dog climbing all over the granite cliffs. We had a slight drama on 'Autumn Flakes' (Hard Severe 4a, 4b, 4b). The guidebook warned us (in bold print!) that "Pitch 3 has been the scene of several serious accidents, due to the leader being unable to follow the correct route".

Unfortunately for us, at the top of Pitch 2, some 100ft up the cliff, we dropped the guidebook while trying to ascertain how to safely navigate through the next pitch! Oops! Luckily, another team had spotted our plight (eventually!) and shouted over some vague directions from a nearby climb and we escaped unscathed.

Bosigran was one of the first Cornish cliffs that I climbed during a week-long trip to the area in 1998. It has all the good ambience of a sea cliff, but with a fraction of the intimidation and faff of those with tidal considerations. Drop something from most sea cliffs and it's consumed by the waters, but with a wide grassy bay at its base and being a safe distance up from the waves, it's a far more forgiving place. The only thing that is unforgiving is the coarse texture of the rough granite, which can soon leave its mark on the soft hands of the uninitiated. It's also a cliff where the routes are generally steep, and the grades are no pushover; something that we seemed to keep forgetting.

From Bosigran, we drove to Sennen. We arrived at 8 pm and found the notorious Mr Moss and Hannah (colleagues from Duchy College) getting ready for a surf. There were only about 15 surfers in the water, the tide was in, and clean green waves were breaking with about a 2ft face. How could we resist? Especially when they produced a 9'2" longboard for me and fins for Clare! Outstanding! We surfed until dark, then followed Mossy to the designated bivi site. We cooked up some simple pasta together by the sea and drank a beer at 11 pm. Perfect.

Sennen Cove is a short distance from Land's End and although famous for its beautiful beach and waves, in the climbing world, it's equally well known for the granite cliffs. These have provided us with plenty of good climbing adventures over the years as well as a memorable day's work for me. Later that summer, I was employed as a safety consultant for a television company, filming for a popular daytime TV show on Channel 4. A job offer that was too good to turn down, despite an already busy schedule.

Helping a camera crew get some clifftop footage, without falling over the edge was easy enough, but the real excitement came when the very keen director wanted the less keen presenter to abseil over the cliff edge. Thankfully, he took it in his stride and didn't require hauling back up again afterwards! I then had to climb a classically photogenic route with one of the contestants of the show. Luckily, he was already an experienced climber, so we were able to get some good footage on some suitably dramatic climbs for the show, rather than having to stage some unrealistic epic. The afternoon's work involved about eight people and after several hours of work, when the show aired, my brief brush with stardom lasted about a minute! Still, I wasn't complaining as it was a nice way to earn some cash, with a lovely bunch of people and with the bonus of being able to go surfing once the work was finished.

Bude, Cornwall
Splendid cliff top layby, SW of Widemouth Bay

June 5th - 6th 2006

LOGBOOK ENTRY:
"A brilliant couple of days/nights. Breakfast, toilet and showers all available at the beach car park. Some great surf too".

This was the ideal van bivi spot. Easy access to the beach, loads of great rock climbing and all facilities available to keep the place from getting trashed. We always aim to 'leave no trace' whenever we van bivi, but sadly you can arrive at spots where other people (not always van users!) have not taken such care. When you find a spot that has access to toilets, bins and maybe even a nearby drinking water tap, it truly is a dream van bivi spot. Being by the sea and near good climbing is, of course, the icing on the cake.

The climbing at Baggy Point provided the scene of multiple adventure routes on steep slabs, but thankfully with plenty of protection. We stayed for a couple of nights, and it provided a great miniature holiday and another fine example of where the Escort van has done us proud. Discreet accommodation for free as well as transport to and from the action.

St Agnes, Cornwall
George's Field

June 26th 2006

LOGBOOK ENTRY:
"Ugh. First day of rain in ages. Literally for about 3 or 4 weeks. Clare has been doing a minibus driving course down here and is due to be camped up here until Thursday. I arrived at about 18:30 and a fine pasta dinner has been prepared. An evening spent reading and discussing the correct distances between a bus mudguard and the road and other such useful nuggets. In between Highway Code trivia, I have been packing and preparing kit for a Peruvian Expedition. Due to be leaving here on Wednesday to begin my journey.
If all goes to plan, I'm meeting Paul tomorrow for a climb or surf, then back here for a farewell dinner with Clare".

George's field felt like one of the last remaining 'traditional' British farmer's campsites in the southwest. Whereas others have grown and developed with business plans, diversified with bike hire and well-stocked camp shops, washing machines and hot tubs, farmer George, a man of indeterminable age, is still keeping it real. A lone tap stands in the corner of the field and a small stone building houses a couple of toilets and a washbasin. And that's it. There's no reception building, no barrier, passcodes, fobs, interrogation on arrival or any form of ID required. You just drive into the field, find somewhere to park and that's it - you're checked in and officially on holiday.

Each morning, George takes a walk around the field and collects his undeniably reasonable rent, cash only. No receipts, printouts, colour map of the site, or menu for the camp takeaway and no questions asked. It's all refreshingly low key and simple – just the way we like our adventures to be. As well as being the regular venue for Walter's (another of my cousins) mid-summer birthday celebrations, we stayed several times when we wanted an easy getaway on the north coast and mid-week, we could often, pretty much have the place to ourselves.

The top corner of the field was the pitch of choice as it was generally a bit flatter and commanded the best views of the ocean. To be fair, the whole field has a magnificent outlook and is drenched in a life-affirming orange hue when the sun dips down into the ocean at the end of the day. The exact location of the field always seemed to escape me and I could never describe it to anyone asking for directions. It's the kind of place that you just learn how to get to. Past the sharp bend, with the old wooden gate; keep going by the house with the red front door and falling down porch; don't be concerned about the strip of grass in the centre of the road – it's still a road; then finally, past the 'almost-too-narrow-for-cars' section and low and behold, turn into the field by the weather-beaten hand-painted 'camping' sign. You've arrived.

Like a lot of the places we've stayed in the van, the best secret spots have only been shared by an introduction or induction from a like-minded traveller. While their exact location is passed on by word of mouth to and from trusted sources, rumours and myths arise to enhance the appeal and mystery. We certainly felt glad that Walter had shared this one with us along with a good percentage of his birthdays.

St Agnes, Cornwall
George's Field

June 27th 2006

LOGBOOK ENTRY:
"Swam with dolphins today! Met Paul at Porthtowan Bay and hired a surfboard as there was a really clean 2ft swell and inland it was too wet to climb. Just the two of us in the water, enjoying some waves, when approximately eight dolphins turned up! After the initial 'shark!' terror response, remembering we were in the UK, we stayed calm and they came within a metre of us and were diving under our surfboards. One for the memory banks".

Participating in outdoor pursuits such as climbing and surfing has always had the happy by-product of allowing me to get to environments that I would otherwise have not thought of going to, or had any need to be operating in. As such, over the years, this has often allowed me to have experiences that most people would not come across in everyday life. Even just being in nature somewhere such as on a mountain top at sunset or in the pre-light of dawn can be a magical experience but interacting with the fauna and flora can add an extra dimension, especially when it's an unplanned or unexpected one.

Lying out on our surfboards, scanning the horizon for the next set of waves, it took quite a while to register what we'd seen heading towards us. Despite the approaching fins, Paul remained much calmer, as I was already paddling frantically for the shore when he called me back. Even with their identification confirmed, I still felt the need to be cautious and it was unsettling to be in the water with creatures so big. As a precaution, I lifted my legs out of the water and knelt on my board, just in case.

The dolphins were more interested in the surf than in us but they stuck around long enough to be inquisitive, diving down underneath our boards, swimming around us and breaking the surface with trademark gracefulness. It was a jaw-dropping experience and one we felt sure no one would believe once we arrived back on the beach. It was certainly a much more intense experience than sitting alongside a crowd of people on a 'whale and dolphin spotting boat', jostling to get the best photo.

With just the two of us in the water, we sat on our boards, open-mouthed, occasionally managing to gasp or whoop. I kept looking around for someone to tell! We were being treated to something that I thought only happened in exotic surf locations. When we eventually returned to shore, we gabbled excitedly at the guys at the surf hire shack. "Wow, that's pretty cool and certainly unusual for this beach," they said, before returning to their job of cleaning wax off old boards. They didn't seem to be particularly excited and I thought, wow if that had been me, I'd be sprinting down the beach to see if they were still there!

I've had the same kind of unenthusiastic reactions before, returning from an expedition, climb or adventure. Unable to contain my excitement, and dying to tell someone what it was like, or what we did, saw or felt, I couldn't believe that they weren't as pumped or desperate to hear more about it. It reinforced the notion that unless you've experienced a situation, it's hard to really know what it's like. It's one of the reasons why experiential learning in outdoor education has always resonated with me.

A few days later, while Clare was passing her PCV Driving test, I arrived in Lima, Peru at the beginning of a journey as the leader of an expedition into the Amazon Jungle. I had led expeditions to many faraway places and had been to Peru before to lead a trek in the Andes but had never set foot inside a tropical rain forest and certainly not one on the scale of the Amazon. It was an educational month away, but I did manage to make a better first impression with the group than my previous time in the high Andes a few years prior. Beset with altitude sickness and dehydration I had passed out while giving a team briefing, with just enough time to ask to be put in the recovery position before slumping to the ground in front of the assembled team.

This time around, there was much more acclimatisation time, which led to some great success in the high mountains, after surviving the rigours of living with spiders and snakes in the jungle phase. I was also lucky enough to have another dolphin encounter and saw some rare 'Pink River Dolphins' swimming next to our boat as we journeyed upstream to our camp in the depths of the Amazon. But that's another story.

Van Life – 2007

Escaping from overnight snowfall
Vanoise National Park, France

Bala, North Wales
Next to the Afon Tryweryn

April 14th 2007

LOGBOOK ENTRY:
"Good to be back in bivi-mode. Seems like ages since I've stretched out in the back of here! I've just been assessed (and passed!) my Level III Whitewater Kayak Coach Assessment. Nice paddling on the river, which was at a good level. Just cooked up. Kit is drying in splendid sunset and it's roasting hot. Feels like the Alps again.
P.S. – Was super cold during the night – Summer Mammut sleeping bag was not sufficient!"

We had by now moved to North Wales because I had secured a job as a teacher of Outdoor Education at St David's College in Llandudno. This required me to not only instruct and guide people in the mountains but also take groups out kayaking. Therefore, I needed to maintain a respectable level of kayaking qualifications.

After my somewhat extreme introduction to the sport as a trainee instructor, my early career saw me spending more and more time in boats. One of the attractions of most outdoor pursuits is that they provide an excellent excuse for travelling to exciting places.

Back in 2001, while at university, I had been part of a kayaking expedition to make first descents of various whitewater rivers in western Kenya. As expected, it provided adventures of the highest order on a daily basis. Being the first kayakers that most of the local population had ever seen, we caused quite a stir wherever we went, and would often have hundreds of villagers lining the riverbanks around a rapid when word got out that we were on our way downstream. This was all before the days of widespread mobile phone use, and it was astonishing to see how fast word could travel in these rural areas.

The expedition involved all sorts of logistical challenges and provided many great lessons in teamwork, communication, kindness and humanity. At the end of the expedition, I had hoped to stay on to earn some money as a raft guide on a commercially guided section of the Tana River, but after a few days of training, it was clear that although I had the necessary skills to read the river and pick a safe line of passage, my scrawny carcass was not going to possess the strength that was required to lever a loaded raft of clients safely downstream and back to their holidays. I decided there and then that I'd leave the rafting business to my barrel-chested friends.

I kept up a decent level of personal kayaking ability but never really pursued the qualifications much further. Until now that is. I did still enjoy guiding people on moderate whitewater rivers and now that I was working full-time as a teacher of Outdoor Education, I decided that I perhaps needed to up my qualifications to the next level. At least the rivers in the UK are a lot less daunting than the fast-flowing, chocolate-brown, wide conveyor belts of African rivers. And there's much less chance of getting taken out by a hungry crocodile, so all in all, it's a much more relaxing day out on a British river.

The van had a roof rack, on which a kayak could be strapped with relative ease (as seen on the front cover of this book). However, I always preferred to keep the boat inside where possible. Not only did this stop drawing attention to the fact that I was likely to have some pinchable kit, but it also meant that driving around was a lot less stressful. With a big plastic lump tied to the roof of the van, there was always the worry that it would detach itself at any point, no matter how many straps and ties were used. That aside, it was more likely that the roof rack and boat would depart as a single unit as the flimsy rusting bolts were always a cause for concern when the boat was hoisted up on top of the van. When the roof rack had to be used, these worries, (compounded by the droning noise created by wind resistance), were usually put to bed with the satisfying and simple solution of just turning the music up a bit louder while on the move.

The kayak assessment, like any test that you feel ready for, involved a couple of days of pure enjoyment. Being away on work time, camped out by a beautiful river and leading people down one of Wales' finest sections of mid-grade rapids was a delight. The river was at a good level and knowing that you are being observed is a good way to ensure that you are at your best and operating with heightened senses. There were four of us being observed and all being of an equal standard, we got on well, despite only having just met. At the debriefs in the campsite, the Escort was dwarfed by the 'bigger vans' with their in-situ beds, cookers and kayak storage areas, but the little van seemed to be getting its fair share of the attention from surprised and amused passers-by who stopped to admire the rig.

To the rear of the van, I sat next to the box-lid table that provided the perfect-sized outdoor kitchen, as well as a good social area once the others joined with their camp chairs. While one guy had a heated drying cupboard in his camper, I had to make do with hanging my wet kayaking kit over a fence to drip dry overnight. Not envious at all.

Metz, France
Service station – Southbound on the péage heading for Austria at the start of a summer of van travels

July 16th 2007

LOGBOOK ENTRY:
"En route to Austria. Pulled into the service station at about 1 am and nestled into a parking spot among the truckers and other van biviers. We rapidly sorted the van into sleep mode and lay down for a surprisingly good sleep. Woke to the alarm. Tired, but need to move on. Fresh air and croissants saw us on our way."

This night's van bivi marked the beginning of an incredible and ambitious summer of van travels that saw us journey across Europe, taking in a range of climbing and mountaineering objectives along the way. Even though we'd only left home four days ago, we'd already had a whirlwind tour of friends and family in the UK that culminated in the kind of day you just couldn't have made up. How better to start a seven week van tour, than with a full-on rock and roll send off, where we ended up backstage with my cousin Wally at the Rhythms of the World music festival in Hertfordshire. Days like that can't be predicted or planned, now and then, they just seem to happen. Money just can't buy that sort of tomfoolery.

The level of planning involved for a climbing trip across Europe, without the aid of modern tools such as google maps, was a feat in itself and the itinerary was pulled together from various articles, photos and descriptions, from well-travelled friends, magazines and the scant amounts of data available on the web. All credit for such logistics goes to Clare, who spent countless hours researching away, producing spreadsheets, budgets and linking routes and roads together.

Incredulous as it seems now, our first major objective was earmarked in a little-known corner of the Austrian Alps. The simple reason being, Clare had found an online climbing topo of a route which had a review saying that it was a classic climb at a reasonable grade. With the topo (a basic route description and sketch showing how to get to the cliff and where the climb goes), downloaded and printed out, all we had to do was drive there. It seemed simple enough while sitting on the sofa in our little terraced house by the Menai Straits. Enthusiasm and the feeling that it would be a good starting point were our motivations. Back then, getting hold of an obscure guidebook was definitely easier once in the country, and we were confident enough that we'd be able to pick up more information on arrival. So, to Austria, we drove, in search of the now much anticipated 'Himmel-Schletter Route'.

The Hochschwab Mountain Hut was the main base to approach the Himmel-Schletter route from. It was a modern hut and the friendly staff helped with translations which resulted in us getting more or less what we thought we'd ordered for dinner. We must have been somewhat of a novelty, as having looked through the 'Hut Book' (where guests sign in), it seemed that not many people from the UK had ever stayed there. Only a few Americans and one person from Canada had in the last two and a half years. Certainly, and somewhat conspicuously, nobody had noted that they had climbed our objective, the (apparently 'classic') South wall of the Hochschwab, as part of their stay.

The wardening of the hut seemed to be a family affair. One of the workers had a battered climbing guidebook and a sketch of the South Wall. Not exactly what we'd expected, as we had naively hoped we'd be able to buy an up-to-date published guidebook from them. Still, they did confirm that the south face had indeed been scaled before and that our rough topo sketch that Clare had printed out from the internet was fairly accurate. The only thing we lacked was a photo of the face to help us locate the base of the route. In broken English and by drawing on our map the Guardian gave us a rough estimate of where he thought the route started.

After breakfast the following morning, we put on harnesses at the hut and set out into the day with a tiny rucksack containing some food, drink and our waterproofs. Our minimalist approach meant we carried the ropes in coils on our backs. During the night the clear skies had clouded over – nothing threatening but a high-level blanket was present well above the mountain tops. It was noted and monitored. The path down to the cliff base skirted around various gullies and then descended further into another valley. Yes, downhill from the hut! We would be climbing back up, over the summit of the peak and then across to the hut. We could soon see the South Wall of the Hochschwab with some faint switchbacks leading up to the foot of the cliff base. Without big packs, we made light work of it and were soon close enough to start locating where to begin from. The features on the cliff face were now beginning to resemble those on our topo and we were pretty sure we had picked out where our intended 'Himmel-Schletter Route' went. Helpfully, there was a vague path in the scree heading up towards the base of it.

It had taken an hour and a half to get to the bottom of the route from the hut and while the clouds stayed high, the wind was picking up. We togged up in waterproofs for warmth before starting upwards. Clare set off first over some lovely slab pitches which had good climbing but were seriously lacking in any protection. There were only two rusty bolts, some bent over pitons and a bolt that had been removed to guide us on our way. I then took over for a semi-traverse with some tricky moves but slightly more in the way of gear. Protection, which came in the form of some slings threaded through water-worn holes in the rock gave a modest level of security.

The next pitches took us through some small overhangs into the massive leftward slanting gully, which was clearly marked on our now very crumpled topo map. All was going well, with nice climbing and us both moving well up the face. But as Clare started to pull up the ropes onto her next belay ledge, the first ominous drops of rain began to fall. This did not bode well. Unseen by us, on the other side of the mountain, huge black cumulonimbus storm clouds had been building all morning and were just about to make their presence known.

I had just reached Clare's belay ledge and we were in the process of switching gear when it all began to kick off. There was a terrifying rumble of thunder that shook the cliff, and then down came the rain in earnest. It was as if a dam had broken above us. We had to move fast and get higher up into the gully with the hope that it would provide some sort of escape route or at least some sort of shelter. I climbed as fast as I could as the rain turned to hail. The crag was soon gushing with water and waterfalls started up out of every crack and crevasse. Miraculously, we found shelter in the form of a small cave that was conveniently positioned higher up in the gully. What a saviour. Clare was quick to join me. We huddled together and discussions ensued. Up? Down? Sit it out and wait? It was impossible to tell from our position. We were well over a hundred metres up the route but there could still be another two hundred meters or so to go. Plus, we didn't know for sure whether this easier gully we now found ourselves near would lead us to the top if we just followed it upwards. Our intended route was due to take us back out onto the exposed face, which was clearly out of the question.

We deliberated over a piece of flapjack while counting the time between the thunder and lightning, which was becoming alarmingly frequent. One, two, three... 'Crash' – then some more eye-burningly bright lightning would follow soon after. Our ribs rattled and vibrated with every jolting peel. The storm was right above us and a pang of fear began to bubble between us. This was the sort of thing you read about in mountaineering books, but here it was, happening to us some hundred metres up a rock face, which was now more like a river. What a place to be stuck in a lightning storm.

So how to get off, was the pressing matter at hand. By following the gully, it did at least look like we would top out and therefore be able to walk back over to the hut. Our now damp and disintegrating topo only had our route drawn on, and the printer ink was beginning to smudge, but there was an arrow pointing in the direction of the gully, with a much lower climbing grade next to it. There was no mention of distance or further obstacles, so we concluded that it could be an escape option. I stuck my head out of the cave and craned my neck upwards to get a feel for the lay of the land.

All plans of utilizing this conveniently placed escape route were quickly put to rest when I was greeted by an assortment of melon-sized rocks which flew noisily down the gully from somewhere up above. Thankfully our sheltered position in the cave meant we were out of the firing line, as the rain seemed to be bringing down anything in its path. The thought of being taken out by a massive rock hurtling down the cliff was now becoming more of a worry than the lightning which seemed to be subsiding. As the storm passed overhead, we sat tight while it moved itself away down the valley. It was not a good situation to be in, but at least we had the shelter of the cave – if the storm had struck when we had been on the exposed slabs, who knows what we would have done or what would have become of us!

So anyway, to continue upwards or begin a retreat down? Neither option was particularly inspiring given our sheltered point. After half an hour or so of cowering in the back of the rock crevice, the hail, which had been steadily accumulating on the ledges around us, turned once again to rain before beginning to ease. Even though the gully above us looked to involve only easy climbing, we decided that climbing upward into the unknown would be foolish. Besides, we had no guide for that route (if it even was one) and were in no mood for new routing opportunities.

The break in the weather gave us our window of opportunity to get down quickly and safely. I belayed Clare down to the previous stance which had a decent looking bolt and hanger which we could begin our descent from. However, no sooner had Clare clipped herself safely in than the heavens re-opened, and the hail flew down from the sky once again. But by now, we were committed.

'Operation Abseil' began once I'd joined Clare and clipped into the same bolts. Hanging side by side from these, with our feet balanced on a small ledge below, we attached some additional small 'maillon' karabiners that were required for the ropes to run smoothly though. We had carried some of these 'back-ups' for this exact reason but had not envisaged placing them in quite such dramatic conditions. We left one on each of the bolts and threaded our ropes through them tying the ends together. We had been climbing using two ropes, which as well as having many advantages of reducing rope drag on the ascent, also meant that with the two ropes tied together, we had a much greater distance range when it came to abseiling back down.

Having descended a rope length and managed to locate the previous belay anchors, I clipped myself in and pressed myself in as close to the rock as possible under a small overhang to avoid any rockfall from above and the worst of the weather. Clare soon joined me and we quickly went about smoothly sorting the ropes in our well-practised way. It's times like this that having a slick system, that needed no discussion, really paid off. With Clare threading the next anchor, I pulled the ropes down, silently praying that they wouldn't get stuck, snagged or bring down a shower of rocks with them. It was an efficient and almost silent operation, with each of us knowing instinctively what to do next. While Clare re-stacked the coils, I was clipping in and preparing to go again. After double-checking each other, we'd load the ropes and go again. This methodical process was repeated a further three times until Clare landed on the screes back at the base of the climb, where we had set off from, seemingly a lifetime ago.

Out of maillons, I had threaded some spare cord onto the last anchor so that the ropes pulled through much easier. Some rapid rope coiling took place as soon as they hit the deck and we ran from the base of the cliff without even taking our rock boots off. When we reached a safe area of grass that was well out of range of any descending rocks we gave each other a look of relief as we dropped our kit and looked back up at where we'd been. The top of the cliff was out of sight in the thick of the clouds and the rock was soaked. It was clear that we'd made the right decision.

The rain still hammered down as I changed my shoes and stuffed some Mars bar into my mouth. As if the rain wasn't enough to deal with, the wind by now had picked up to gale force levels making it difficult to stand up straight and immediately stole any heat that we were generating. Just to add to the drama, the thunder and lightning started back up as we set off towards the hut. It was only a matter of minutes before our feet began squelching around inside our soaking shoes. After walking down to a junction in the path, the rain eased for a few minutes but with the thunder and a new wave of rain approaching there was a distinct sense of urgency to get back up to the hut.

We put our heads down and arrived in an hour less than the signposted time. As the sanctuary of the building loomed into view, the hut guardians who had given us information about the route gingerly poked their heads out of the windows and gave us a friendly wave. The wind slammed the door shut behind us and we both just stood in the entrance hallway exhaling sizable breaths of relief that we had made it back safely. Only minutes before, the driving rains had stung our eyes making it hard to see where we were going but now in the warmth of the porch, all was quiet and calm. Dripping all over the floorboards, it was a huge relief to take off our harnesses and the ropes that hung heavily from our shoulders. We stripped off virtually everything, carefully hanging our kit in the drying room amongst many other wet boots and jackets. In the main room, the Guardian presented us with a jug of hot water to make tea with and sheepishly seemed to be saying that the storm had not been forecast. As best we could, we told our tale of adventure while warming up.

The following day, the weather was only slightly better. Not good enough for a rematch with the Himmel-Schletter Route, but good enough for us to make an ascent on foot to the huge wooden cross that marks the top of the Hochswab at 2277m. The views came and went between the clouds as we scribbled our names into the summit book. Perhaps one day we'd return to climb here again, but for now, we had the long walk back to the valley and the awaiting van.

From Austria, we crossed into Slovenia, via a very remote and high mountain pass that was generally deemed by us to be unsuitable terrain for an Escort van. The scenery, however, was stunning and the route saved us many miles on our journey to visit another of my cousins, Nancy.

Nancy and Stu, who had moved to Slovenia a couple of years before, hosted us for a few days in their mountain chalet in the woods. Via a few expensive 'international text messages' a rendezvous was arranged, and we met them in their nearest town. After picking up a few provisions and marvelling at their ability to converse with the locals, we followed their 'tank' (a well-used Russian 4x4 Jeep) along rough gravel roads through miles and miles of thick forest. Their choice of vehicle was much more suited to the terrain than our tired van. We did our best to keep up with them while maintaining a safe distance behind the billowing clouds of dust that they were leaving in their wake. Hot, sweaty and choking on dust, we eventually arrived to a very warm welcome at their incredible home in the heart of a Slovenian forest.

Mojstrana, Slovenia
Kamp Kamne

July 30th 2007

LOGBOOK ENTRY:
"€13.50 for a very quiet and chilled campsite. Arrived late with no motivation to faff with the tent – especially as the ground is wet and we are due to be leaving early (weather permitting) for an ascent of Triglav in the morning – Slovenia's highest mountain. Cold outside, but feeling snug in here. Candles lit and iPod on. Luxury".

After a few days of rock climbing, trekking and swimming around Lake Bled and the town of Bohinj, the van had led us to the base of Triglav – the highest peak in Slovenia and a great looking objective for anyone in search of a mountaineering adventure. It seemed that the more we saw of the country, the more possibilities and places to explore kept appearing. While an ascent of Triglav was high on our list, we still had to decide which route we would climb. The Slovenians have a long and rich heritage of mountaineering, with a running theme that seems to involve an attraction to long dangerous routes through questionable terrain. Having read through some of the route descriptions, the steep walls of Triglav seemed to be home to plenty of these.

The North Face route seemed to offer an acceptable balance of interest, difficulty, adventure and safety. It was mostly walking and scrambling, but through very exposed terrain, which is equipped in places with wires and chains to offer a degree of security. A well-positioned hut (or 'Dom' as they are known in Slovenia), meant that rest could be had before making a summit bid up the final knife-edge ridge the following day.

Arriving in the van below the great north wall was exciting enough and we took a day to check out the local area and acclimatise a bit. The mountain looked huge and the cliffs and crags that towered up above us seemed to offer no obvious way through them. Whoever had made the first ascent must have been an excellent route finder and certainly much braver than me. We cooked up by the banks of a beautiful river with deep turquoise waters and would have quite liked to have stayed the night there, but it didn't feel quite right. Instead, we slowly bumped our way a further ten kilometres down a rough track that was masquerading as an actual road, to a large wooden Dom. Given that the weather was threatening to turn a little on the damp side, we decided to treat ourselves to a night indoors.

It was very dark inside and not particularly busy, which given the state of the road that led there, was no particular surprise. There was a poster with a list of alpine clubs and walking groups from all over the world pinned to the wall by the reception desk, which seemed to be promoting the offer of a fifty per cent price reduction to all affiliates. Sadly, no British groups were represented. Unperturbed, our British Mountaineering Council and my International Mountain Leaders card were confidently placed on the counter. After scrutinizing them as if authenticating a cut diamond or rare stamp, the warden eventually wrote a figure on her pad of paper and slid it silently across to us. It bore no resemblance to any of the advertised prices but was well over the half-price discount. We handed over the Euros quickly before she could change her mind.

'Bargain' we thought as we followed the lady through the dim light and up the creaking wooden staircase. The delight in scoring our cheapest accommodation yet was short-lived as it was soon to also gain the less auspicious title of our worst accommodation yet. We were taken to the top of the building, where a communal dorm had been established. By established, I mean that a few thin, filthy mattresses had been scatted on the floor under the eaves and a small sign reading 'dorm' had been unevenly screwed to the door. There was just enough headspace to walk down the middle of the room, without standing on a couple of German trekkers who were already in residence. At the far end, where we were directed, emanated a terrible smell, so we took the side that at least had a skylight and the chance of some fresh air.

As we lay down to sleep, we assured ourselves that the rodents that were running noisily around the attic were probably not rats and 'only' mice. We tried to go to sleep as fast as possible, feeling very squeamish, but knowing it would be a short night as we planned to be back at the van before first light. At least we hadn't paid much for the privilege of this wonderful sleep. Nights like that make you appreciate the van even more. The inside of the van might get a bit messy, but at least it is our mess – and there were no dead or rotting rodents hidden inside! Ugh! A night best forgotten about.

Mojstrana, Slovenia
Kamp Kamne

July 31st 2007

LOGBOOK ENTRY:
"Wow! Check us out! Alpine Stars! We were so fast climbing Slovenia's highest peak, that we decided to climb it in a single day, rather than the normal two days. 10 hour round trip van to van with 1850m of vertical ascent and descent! Back at the Van Basecamp by 20:45. Tea, biscuits, a few stretches, then sleep! A big day out."

The North Face Route of Triglav was every bit as exciting as it had looked from the forest when we arrived in the area a few days ago. It was an enjoyable hike and scramble that took us to the mountain hut and our initially planned stop for the night.

As we approached the high mountain hut, and as if to ensure we knew we were somewhere a little bit different, we were greeted by a lady singing a traditional Slovenian verse at the top of her voice outside the hut. The sound of her accompanying accordion player, drifted across the mountainside before we caught sight of the actual building. What she lacked in musical ability she was certainly making up for with enthusiasm. It was early in the afternoon and we were still reeling from our recent night in a Slovenian mountain hut. Perhaps another could be avoided?

The final summit ridge on Triglav is an impressive crest, with large drops on either side and marred only by the fact there is a line of rickety metal posts and chains lining the way. From the terrace of the hut, it looked close enough to go for. It was still early and neither of us fancied hanging around another dark wooden building, especially one with a strange operatic lady in residence so we decided to take on the summit rather than checking into the hut.

It wasn't until we reached the top of the mountain that we realised the traditional summit ritual wasn't just a windup. As well as it being every Slovenian's duty to climb to the highest point in the country, we had also been told that once on top, every summiteer should receive a spanking from a birch branch. It sounded highly implausible to me.

Looking a bit like a rocket ready for launch, the conical metal summit shelter was deserted when we made our final steps of ascent, so we had the chance to take in the views by ourselves. After a while another couple crested the final ridge and made their way over to us, looking equally pleased with themselves. It's not unusual to be asked to take a summit photograph of another team and it's a request that can be made without much need for a shared language as a bit of sign language is normally enough to get the message across.

On the summit of Triglav, in reasonably good but broken English, the request seemed to be asking for more than a photo. *"Would you mind spanking my wife while I take a photograph?"* seemed to be the result of the first round of translation charades. We must have looked confused and a little perturbed at the ask, and eventually, the realisation began to dawn that perhaps we had not been the victims of a wind-up. They tried again, *"would you mind taking a photograph of my wife as she gives me a good spanking on the summit?"* This seemed slightly less kinky and marginally less weird. They seemed as sincere as someone asking for directions to the post office, so we had no choice but to oblige. Despite our slowness to cotton on to what they wanted, we had at least been forewarned about this tradition. To our new friends, the request seemed a perfectly normal thing to do on the nation's highest peak in the middle of the Julian Alps and in no way an error in translation.

Returning to the hut after our unusual summit experience, we decided that we still had enough energy to get back to the valley, so saved the fees of another hut night and arrived triumphant back at the van, knees shaking from the 1800m of ascent and descent, just before dark. A big day.

Not only was climbing Triglav an enjoyable day out it was also interesting to see the difference in ethics in the mountains. British mountaineers would have been aghast at the brushstrokes of red paint that had been dabbed and circled on rocks to guide climbers every few metres, almost all the way to the summit. We were used to seeing some carefully placed and immaculately painted red signs in the Alps, but this was on a different level entirely! And if the blatant graffiti wasn't shocking enough to our ethic of 'leaving no trace', anywhere that the trail crossed a tricky rock step or awkward ground, someone had either chiselled a step or cemented in a convenient chain handrail.

We laughed and marvelled at the work that had gone into creating the route, as much as at the difference in mountaineering ethics that you encounter across the world. It was a stark contrast to the paths on the mountains in the United Kingdom, and we wondered what the reaction would be if someone had done the same up the north ridge of Tryfan. I believe the British Mountaineering Council and outdoor community would be up in arms!

Despite the liberal use of route markings and assistance with some of the trickier sections, there was no getting away from the size and exposure of Slovenia's highest peak, both of which were fantastic.

West Coast, Croatia
Nudist Camp

August 3rd 2007

LOGBOOK ENTRY:
"Arrived in the dark. Went to sleep under a big moon – and woke to find a few more! Saw so much more than we expected! Made a prompt red-cheeked departure!"

Croatia in August is a very hot place to be. Croatia in August, inside an Escort Van, involved temperatures that my body had rarely encountered before. If one thing remained constant during our time in the country, it was the fact that we were sweating throughout our entire stay. However, despite the potentially inhospitable summer temperatures, according to our research, Croatia also seemed to be home to some excellent rock climbing areas and it was the pull of these which drew us to the area.

As well as rock climbing, we soon realised by way of happy discovery, that there was an ease of access to several of the coastal regions. Here was the chance to cool off in the clear warm waters – something that was often needed several times a day. Being the prepared travellers that we were, in the back of the van we happened to be carrying some snorkelling gear, so we spent quite a bit of time happily exploring the beaches and coastline looking for new areas to keep cool on our way down to our target destination of Paklenica Gorge.

So far on our journey through Croatia it had been made clear, not only by signs but by the fact that we had been moved on by the police one evening, that to van bivi in undesignated areas was strictly forbidden. Rather than stay in our current idyllic layby, we felt inclined to push on down the coast in search of an official campsite. Having already eaten and with the sun having long since set, all we had to do was sleep. After seeing a camping symbol on a faded wooden sign, we followed a dusty track down to the water's edge figuring that we'd just park up, sleep, and sort out payments in the morning. The proximity to the sea gave anticipation of a morning swim, so having found a flat spot and admired the full moon, we climbed into the back and slept.

It's always interesting waking up at a camp spot when you arrived at night because you never really know what it will be like until you see it in daylight. We were greeted with a little more than we expected!

Seeing the odd topless swimmer or naked sunbather is pretty standard stuff on the beaches of Europe, so we were slow to realise it wasn't just the odd swimmer going au-naturel. We were certainly off the beaten track, parked as we were, on a deserted strip of coastline, we just hadn't realised in the dark that we'd parked up in the centre of a nudist camp.

Having obliviously flung open the backdoors to let in some cooler air and the bright light of day, we dashed down to the sea for a morning dip. After diving in, we looked back to be greeted with a friendly wave from the group of bronzed holidaymakers, who were all hanging out (literally!) by the water's edge, clearly working on their all-over tan.

Paklenica, Croatia
Camping Marko

August 8th 2007

LOGBOOK ENTRY:
"The hottest night. Enough said... 'Phew' - No covers, no clothes, doors wide open"

Climb, sweat, snorkel, climb, repeat. Over the next few days, we worked out a routine that allowed us to both survive and enjoy our situation. It was too hot to contemplate sleeping in an oven-like tent in the given temperatures, but luckily once the fierce power of the sun reduced, the van cooled down sufficiently to allow us to sleep. Although clothes were allowed at this campsite, it was too hot to be covered with more than the bare minimum to remain decent.

It seems bonkers these days that we travelled across Europe under the stifling summer heat, in a vehicle that was not equipped with air-conditioning. On the other hand, looking back it's also easy to see how. I guess two factors influenced this. The first is that we'd not spent a huge amount of time driving on the continent in summer and the second is that I'd never actually owned another vehicle so had no idea that an air-conditioned cab could be so comfortable on a long journey!

Driving along, with the air blowers on full blast, we'd be getting 'cooled down' by air that was the same temperature as the outside air - often well into the thirty-degrees Celsius range. It was usually a pretty sweaty affair, but when you don't know any better, it seems fine. However, it usually wasn't long before the engine needed cooling even more than we did. Driving on the hottest days, we'd nervously be eyeing the temperature gauge as it crept slowly towards the red. The need to shift heat from the ever-warming engine often required immediate and drastic action and our best solution would be to turn the dashboard heat up full to try and draw away the heat from the mechanics of the engine. This was very effective at cooling things under the bonnet, but only really transferred the problem to the cab, where life-threatening temperatures would be getting created as the red-hot air was pumped into the front of the van.

To combat this, the front windows were wound fully down to release the build-up of heat. It was actually pretty effective, but arriving at our destination, we'd always still exit the front doors having peeled ourselves out of the sweaty seats, with damp shirts stuck to our backs. And that's how we covered a lot of summer miles. Windows down, heaters on full, and the radio turned up as high as we could to drown out the sound of the road rushing by.

On one particularly hot drive in Croatia, we stopped to rest the van, lining it up under a small patch of shade. We knocked it out of gear and applied the handbrake as usual, but it took a few moments to realise that something was amiss. It was only halfway out of the driver's door, with the van key in hand, it dawned on us that the engine was still running! How you stop a van that has had the key removed was a question that neither of us had an immediate answer to. Letting the engine idle until it ran out of diesel didn't seem like the most efficient answer and would only lead to the problem of needing to source more fuel to get it going again, so we climbed back in, re-inserted the key and moved it back and forth, but the same problem remained. In the end, Clare decided to stall the engine and all three of us seemed to breathe a sigh of relief. Thankfully, this turned out to be a one-off anomaly and not our standard parking technique for the remainder of the expedition.

Mornings had to start early in Croatia, whether we were tired or not and despite our frequent reluctance to get going, motivation came from the knowledge that in the delicious cool of the shady morning, climbing was actually both possible and pleasant. With a guidebook stocked full of routes, there was plenty to climb. As well as trying to pick the best routes we would also carefully select them based on aspect and avoidance of direct sunlight. Whereas earlier in the expedition, in the mountains of Austria, we had climbed big routes, with a rucksack full of spare clothes and waterproofs, here I climbed shirtless and with a pack containing only water and a few bites of food. Away from the valley floor, there tended to be a bit of a breeze, but it often felt like a race against the sun as we worked our way upward until the heat would prevent any further progress.

Usually, before midday, we'd be back on the ground, walking out against the flow of tourists who flocked noisily into the gorge. In the van, we'd drive the few minutes down the road to a quiet jetty that we'd found at the coast, then dive straight into the cooling waters. An enjoyable mix of snorkelling and climbing came to provide a happy routine for a few days.

Paklenica, Croatia
Camping Marko

August 9th 2007

LOGBOOK ENTRY:
"Climbed two 150m routes during the day - both with grippingly wide traverses over huge drops which gave an extra 'exposure pump'. To add to the already heightened states of anxiety, thunder rumbled around the gorge all day, although the real storm didn't hit until we were safely back at camp. Lightning flashed continuously for over two hours while the rain fell heavily. Safely tucked up in the van, with the awning up, we drank coffee, played cards and talked while watching the lightning. Slept with the doors open and the porch up. Brilliant."

A break in the weather seemed inevitable at some point. The oppressive heat had been building all week and was destined to be released via a big thunderstorm before long. Although we'd both always pick sunshine over rain, I think we were both ready for a cooling of the temperatures and the only way that that was likely to happen was with a downpour. The only thing we didn't want, was to be caught out, high up on an exposed cliff when it happened.

The sky was a different colour when we set out into the dim light of the day. The bright blue that we had become accustomed to had been replaced by a deeper haze of high-altitude clouds, reducing the colour of the dawn and preventing the usual rays of sun from lighting up the cliffs of Anica Kuk on the opposite side of the gorge. The weather was changing, that much was for sure. What we didn't know, was at what speed. We still had a few big climbs that we fancied trying, so we set off cautiously, moving as fast as the terrain allowed. As usual, we swung leads to keep an efficient rhythm of movement as we climbed.

When out on lead, it was easy to get absorbed in the technicalities of the climbing. Finding handholds, moving between bolts, checking the route and simply hanging on, were more than enough to occupy the mind. Especially with the added handicap of sweat dripping into your eyes. But during my turn hanging from a belay stance, my eyes would be scanning the horizon behind us and my good ear eagerly tuning into the distant sound of thunder. Clipped to a chain that was anchored to the rock by two drilled bolts, we would hang back in the comfort of our climbing harness with the spare rope coiled neatly in front of us ready to pay out to whichever one of us was climbing next. Below us was nothing but air until the ground, some 100m below. The climbs were fabulously exposed, but we were very much aware that they offered nothing in the way of shelter.

Distant rumbles of thunder on the horizon would soon be making landfall, but unlike the alpine storm, we were grateful that they seemed to be in no great rush to arrive. Clouds were certainly building, and the rumbles were increasingly audible, but from what we deemed a safe distance. It was as if we were being permitted to finish our climb. Sweaty and sticky from a combination of the humidity and fast climbing, we reached the final anchor. Barring any rope jamming abseil fiasco, it looked like we were not going to have to relive our recent dramatic thunderstorm experience. The ropes ran smoothly, and we were safely back at camp as the raindrops and temperature began to fall in unison.

Osp, Slovenia
Camping Vork

August 10th – 12th 2007

LOGBOOK ENTRY:
"Northwest Slovenia, near the Italian Border. Turns out it's quite a mecca for those with much stronger arms than us. Climbing sport routes at Crini Kal and getting pumped arms on consecutive '6a' graded routes. A night with the van here cost €7.50 and the owner (also a climber with sausage-sized fingers), has sold us some homemade wine for €3.50. Very nice."

Some Slovenian climbers that we had met earlier on the expedition had given us directions to the crags of Osp, with the advice that they can be a good bet when the weather is poor elsewhere. As Croatia looked to be washed out for a few days, we decided to move on and check it out. The reports were correct, and the climbing was really good, but also really hard. It was one of the friendliest places that we had visited and the locals seemed to appreciate the fact that a couple of crazy British climbers had driven their van all the way across Europe to check it out.

The campsite owner very kindly lent us a guidebook to the crag and we climbed plenty of routes in between marvelling at the Slovenians who were walking up some of the hardest routes we'd ever seen. The standard of fitness and stamina of the local climbers was astonishing, especially given the amount of wine they were capable of consuming in the evenings. There were quite a few climbers who had moved there for the summer to 'work' on various projects and unclimbed lines. Having been introduced to climbing with the traditional ethic of, either you can climb it or you can't, this style of climbing had never really appealed to us, but it was interesting to see a different approach. The climbing scene really has a remarkable variety of practices and ethics.

For me, the repetitive practising of each move on a climb to gradually piece together an ascent holds little allure. I can get into it while trying to work out how to climb a boulder problem but on a longer route, the achievement and satisfaction generally come from arriving at the base and puzzling out a way to the top without falling off. This is known as a 'ground-up' or an 'on-sight' ascent and is usually my preference. In the wonderful world of climbing, there are many different genres, ethics and styles which make up the various facets of the sport. Because you're only really competing against yourself, you can climb a cliff in the style that suits you best. In other sports, such as cycling, kayaking or skiing, it's possible to employ better or more advanced equipment to create marginal gains in performance, but I like the fact that generally, in climbing, you can either hold on, or you can't.

The only consistent etiquette in climbing is that you're honest about your style of ascent. No one likes a bragger or a blagger after all.

Trieste, Italy
Camping Aquileia

August 13th 2007

LOGBOOK ENTRY:
"A quick stopover – we're actually a bit further north of Trieste and tomorrow we are taking the train west into the city of Venice, where the sheer luxury of crisp white cotton sheets on a large double bed awaits! Had a dip in the pool before dinner and had to hire comedy red swimming hats to be allowed entry! Everyone else seemed to have their own. What's that all about!? Still, at least Speedos were not a prerequisite!"

Ah, Venice! The city of romance! This really was a holiday from a holiday and a surreal break from life in the wild to some serious city spoils! With the van abandoned in a random Italian town, we nervously left it parked up on a discreet backstreet and walked down to the nearby train station, hoping that it would still be there, along with its contents, on our return in a few days. With just a light rucksack between us, unencumbered by a van and all our possessions, we were transported into a different world. The city of Venice, from what we could make out, was no place to try and drive into, so we relaxed into the novelty of having the train navigate us directly into the central station.

It was an excellent way to arrive as having disembarked, you are instantly thrust into the midst of the iconic surrounds of canals, bridges and gondolas. One of the biggest culture shocks for us was being around so many people – the noise of the city and its inhabitants flooded our senses as the train doors slid open. Having spent the last month or so frequenting empty valleys and quiet mountain ranges, it was exciting to be in amongst a crowd. We found ourselves being drawn to watching people almost as much as the buildings and architectural skyline.

Given that cities like this were generally off the scale in terms of affordability, it was a big decision to stomach the vast expense of a hotel stay. Via some enquiries at the tourist office on arrival, we found something in the vague region of our minimal budget that totalled about the same cost as our previous week of expenses. But it was only a short walk away from the station and inside provided an oasis of quiet and calm in the form of our own private space. We could have spent the whole day luxuriating in the cleanliness of the spacious air-conditioned room. But, given that we were in Venice and on a time limit of a few days, after freshening up, we set back out into the throng.

The strange thing about Venice is that even though almost all the buildings are in a dreadful state of repair and collapse, they all still retain an aura of class and beauty. There can't be many towns in the world where derelict areas have tourists flocking to them to take photographs and pose in front of falling-down doorways or boarded-up windows. Liverpool, the city where I studied for my undergraduate degree has plenty of run-down districts that fit this description, but it's just not quite the same. Venice is in a class of its own.

We lost ourselves in the maze of bridges, alleyways and arches, trying only to use the map periodically to check our bearings. All paths seemed to eventually lead to the centrepiece of St Mark's Square and the distance from it seemed to be in direct proportion to the price of everything on sale. A drink that cost one euro near the station, was guaranteed to be at least five euros by the time you were in the main square. To be fair, the main square is an extraordinary place to sit down and enjoy a coffee, but economics encouraged us to take a seat at any number of the lesser known, but equally stunning nearby piazzas, where our meagre budget would stretch much further. Naturally, pizza was on the menu for dinner and Clare's diligent research directed us to what was billed as the best pizza in Venice – we were inclined to agree. Along with a few other guidebook tip-offs, her plans helped us to enjoy all that the city had to offer, before collapsing at last into the comfort of a real bed.

Northern Italy
North of the Dolomites, near the Austrian Border

August 20th 2007

LOGBOOK ENTRY:
"Super nice, small camp spot. Modern, clean facilities! Almost luxury van camping! Unbelievably, it snowed last night, so climbing is now out of the question. Stopped at Sellajoch and viewed the famous Sella Towers through the binoculars, but very misty and raining – snow covering the tops anyway! Time to run away in search of better weather.
But, we did discover an amazing pizza restaurant with the best wine and coffee of the trip! Mega! Somehow our feast only came to €19.00! Cheers Italy!"

An unexpected late summer covering of snowfall across the central Alps, coupled with a general feeling of fatigue from life on the road, signalled the beginning of the end of the summer's mountain-based adventures. During the previous week, we had enjoyed a brief taste of some of the delights that the towering Dolomiti rock climbing had to offer and we were very keen for more, but the weather had other ideas. It was an area of the Alps that I had heard so much about and as soon as we arrived, we'd set straight out to try one of the famous '*Via Ferratas*' that wind their way up improbably steep and wild mountain terrain.

While a lot of fun, they didn't seem to hold the same draw as climbing a peak without the assistance of the steps, staples and chains, lining the way. Our guidebook of classic climbs listed no shortage of adventurous options and on closer inspection, only seemed to offer very long adventurous options! Climbing in the Dolomites would generally involve two major factors. One was that the routes were likely to be serious, long and committing, with at least one section of loose rock to negotiate (especially if you wanted to avoid paying for a cable car). The second was the seemingly constant threat of afternoon thunderstorms, of which we were now wise enough to be sufficiently cautious.

Before the falling snow put an end to the plans, we enjoyed some good climbing to plenty of impressive summits and had a list of other peaks to return to for another day. An afternoon spent climbing at a single pitch venue near Cortina only served to accentuate that the good stuff was up high and now out of bounds for a while. Subsequently, we packed up camp and set off to Basel in Switzerland where we knew a friend of ours lived.

We have been lucky enough that through climbing, work and studies we have met and made friends from all around the world, or at least met ones that have since moved to exciting places. These friends, often tend to be the ones who, while we don't see them very often, are always there at the end of a phone or ready to drop everything when they hear you are unexpectedly in town.

An email was sent, giving our friends about twenty-four hours' warning of our arrival in Switzerland and after getting lost through a few sets of diversions on the freeway, we were greeted with friendly hugs and handshakes in the designated meeting bar in Basel. A whirlwind of stories, sights and first-class hosting from Jim and his friends, gave a wonderful finale to the summer expedition.

Over the years, I've had some fabulously random meetups and nights out that have been instigated by a single text or email and have resulted in ridiculous levels of hospitality and generosity. *"You get yourself here, and we'll sort the rest"* is the unwritten rule.

A fine example of this came about after waving off a group that I had been leading on a month-long expedition in the little-known mountains of Malawi in Africa a few years prior. I still had another month until I was due to return to the UK and had loosely planned on exploring more of the country by myself. But for various reasons, after four weeks I was keener to move on and visit somewhere different.

At the airport, with bags already packed and having said my goodbyes to the team, I went over to the ticket desk to see what options might be available to me. I soon found out that there was a plane bound for Nairobi, Kenya on the runway and ready to leave. For a reasonable fee, they were willing to get me on board. It was a surreal moment, but for some reason, I decided to go for it. Usually, I am much more inclined to weigh up several options and think about the pros and cons of each, but the spontaneous adventure of it all sparked something inside me and before I knew it, I had handed over my credit card and been escorted to the runway.

The plane was already on the tarmac with engines running as I was whisked across from the terminal to give my rucksack to the baggage guy.

As I got to the top of the steps and boarded, a flight attendant closed the door behind me while another ushered me quickly to my seat to prevent the flight from leaving any later than I'd already made it.

We were up in the air before I knew what was going on. I had intended to make a plan for my arrival in Nairobi during the flight, but once seated, a sudden wave of exhaustion came over me. The relief of finally not being responsible for a whole group of people lifted off my shoulders, allowing my eyelids to weigh down over my eyes. I sank back into the seat and drifted into a deep sleep.

I awoke, with a dry mouth and sleep crusted eyes as the captain announced our imminent arrival in Kenya. As I regained consciousness, I was surprised to find that it was pitch black outside. All I could see from the small window were scattered lights, indicating the city limits below as we closed in on the runway. At the time, solo travel was not something that was recommended around Nairobi (often dubbed as Ni-robbery) and doing so after dark was to be avoided where at all possible. That we would be arriving in darkness was not something that I had considered while in the bright light of the Malawian sunshine earlier that afternoon. I needed to make a plan, and fast.

Having been to Nairobi before, I did have a couple of friends who lived there but only had an email address and no phone number to contact them. I didn't even know their physical address. The rough, and what was transpiring to be, an ill-thought-out plan that I had hurriedly envisaged as I booked the plane ticket, was that I'd get a bus into the centre of town, from where I'd probably remember how to get to James' house. What I hadn't considered was the travel time that this would take to achieve, or that it would be well past the hour that a lone foreign traveller should be a) on a bus and b) in the centre of Nairobi. The airport is a decent way out of the city, but using the unofficial local 'Matatu' minibuses, I figured that it should only cost about fifty pence - a pound at most. But now, it seemed, I was going to have to take a taxi, a safer solution, but one that was destined to be vastly more expensive and also not without its risks in the dark of night.

I determined to see if I could convince a fellow traveller to share a taxi. This would help by reducing the burden of the fare as well as providing some perceived safety in numbers. In the terminal, as the baggage came off the carousel, I began pitching my idea to anyone who looked like a reasonable travel companion. After disappointingly receiving a good number of replies in the negative, I caught sight of my bearded reflection in the glass divider in the middle of the conveyor belt. I had on my 'cleaner' set of clothes from my limited wardrobe of the previous month, but I was not looking clean by any stretch of the imagination, especially when you factored in the wild hair and unkempt beard. I wasn't entirely sure that I would want to get in a taxi with me!

With just a few travellers left waiting for their bags, things were not looking in my favour. The last woman I asked was particularly well dressed and certainly an unlikely companion for the dusty tramp that approached her. Naturally, she wasn't looking to share a taxi, but for whatever reason, took pity on me, and for that, I will be eternally grateful. The reason that she didn't need a taxi was that she had a 'driver' waiting for her outside in a very smart looking jet-black Land Rover with smoked-out windows. I could scarcely believe my luck.

We were heading towards the city as I entertained my new hosts with the ill-thought-through details of my half-baked plan. The driver was insistent that I should not be dropped off in the centre of town at that time of night, but I had to sheepishly admit that I didn't exactly know where my friends lived and that they were unaware I was even in Kenya. Although I didn't know the exact address, I did remember a nearby street name and was relatively sure that I'd be able to navigate myself from there. Amazingly, the driver recognised the street name and after some slow trawling of the neighbourhood, my memories matched up with reality and with much relief, I successfully located James' house.

Thanking my saviour and her driver, I rang the bell and after a nervous wait on the doorstep, I was welcomed into the open arms of the disbelieving occupants! I was given fresh, (if completely ill-fitting) clothes and after being fed, was taken out for a wild night of impromptu partying. Several weeks of kayak and raft-based adventures with the guys ensued and culminated with an even more eventful overland return journey through East Africa back to Malawi, but I'm digressing into an entirely different story.

Saint-Omer, France

Northbound service station 40km south of Boulogne

August 23rd 2007

LOGBOOK ENTRY:
"Back on the 'Péage' Toll Road. Stopped for a final cook-up in a picnic area in the services before this one. Arrived here at about 23:00 and got straight into the back to sleep. Over the water to the Dover at 09:00 the next morning, so up and out at 07:00 - made coffee and breakfast in the queue for the ferry."

A tactical overnight stop-off in the service station that came to be one of our 'regular' van bivies over the years. Organising the back of the van into sleep mode has been dialled down to such an art, that it feels like somewhere in between an episode of Transformers and a military operation. Everything has a place and is slotted neatly and efficiently into it – including us. A basic, but essentially hassle-free, cheap night and one that served us well over the years. Cooking dinner in a picnic area before arrival ensures the smoothest of operations and is well recommended.

Van Life – 2008

Off-road in the Picos de Europa, Spain

Troyes, France

Southbound service station, near Troyes, heading for a ski touring adventure.

March 23rd 2008

LOGBOOK ENTRY:
"Epic journey through blizzards and snow! Left Fort Martin covered in a few centimetres of snow, but on arrival in Boulogne, found more like 30cm in depth and traffic chaos. Took two and a half hours to travel the first 20 kilometres into France. Not a good start to a 1000km trip!"

For several years, the van provided us with reliable travel to Europe's alpine regions to enjoy various ski touring expeditions, often with a bit of rock climbing thrown in for good measure. Our tried and tested formula would involve leaving home in Wales at the earliest opportunity and crossing the channel on a cheap late-night ferry. Once in France, we'd continue a short distance, until fatigue would force us to stop at a service station and we'd bed down in the back of the van among the ski kit. To maximise space, if we had the energy, the skis were hoisted up into the roof using a web of cords. Otherwise, we'd just snuggle up with them.

The following day would usually be enough to see us arrive at our intended alpine destination, usually somewhere such as Switzerland, Austria or France. A bunkhouse or small apartment would be utilised for a few days, while we got ski fit and acclimatised. Then we would set out on a ski journey in the high mountains, moving between the network of mountain huts. Our previous experiences of winter van bivies in the alps had convinced us that having a warm room, hot shower and drying facilities is worth the extra expense.

Sometimes ski touring we would travel just as a pair, and on other occasions, we would be joined by friends. As well as the satisfaction of completing a journey, the ability to choose where to go gives a much more rewarding and enjoyable experience than skiing on the pre-groomed pistes in a resort area. I like cruising down a well-groomed run as much as anyone, but as those who have skied off-piste will know, the difference in the feeling as you silently sink and rise in and out of a turn in deep powder, is both pleasing and addictive. Being able to get to those pristine, untouched powder snow fields is part of the magic of ski touring.

This particular journey saw us heading slowly through a slightly stressful and snow-covered central France, in the direction of the Vanoise National Park. Here we planned to have a few days skiing by ourselves before meeting the Jepson family and friends to embark on a ski tour from the village of Aussois.

We had timed our arrival in the Vanoise well. After the big dump of snow that had hampered our progress driving to the mountains, things had calmed down which allowed us to reach some peaks and cols while ski touring on mostly fresh snow. Apart from one very windy day, we had favourable conditions.

It's a wonderful feeling setting out on the start of a journey on skis. As you shuffle up into the mountains you become absorbed in the environment. Thoughts and concentrations can all be focused on the route, the snow, the terrain and the weather, blissfully away from everyday normal life.

There was a range of hut experiences on this trip, including one unmanned one, which required us to melt snow in a huge pot on top of the wood burner for drinking water. Luckily the rest had a guardian and running drinking water. This generally meant a more luxurious night with the bonus of having someone cook you dinner when you get there. However, not all huts are made equal and one became the tour favourite.

On approach to this hut, we found an untracked slope of dry, fluffy powder snow. Perfect conditions and everybody enjoyed putting in beautiful tracks. It was so good, we skinned back up to do it all over again!

There were fresh ski tracks on the approach to the hut, and when we eventually arrived, we discovered that they belonged to the hut guardian, who had skied up from the village that morning carrying fresh food ready for our arrival!

Tim declared that the skiing had been so good, that he felt duty-bound to buy us all a round of beers, which we gratefully enjoyed on the snowy terrace looking out at the slope that held our recently etched tracks. The hut soon became our favourite and not just because it had a toilet located inside the building! After a filling meal of soup and pasta, the guardian produced a fresh fruit chocolate fondue. Outstanding culinary skills, from a rudimentary kitchen at somewhere around 2500m on a remote mountainside!

Cormot, France
Cormot Crag Car Park

April 3rd 2008

LOGBOOK ENTRY:
"After a triumphant 1600m ski descent through untracked powder snowfields in the Vanoise Massif, we got straight into the van and drove north, stopping only for road tolls and a quick boulangère session. Initial estimates suggested that we should arrive at the 'Club Alpine Français' Hut in the village of Cormot at about 20:30."

We certainly packed a lot into our time in the mountains. It was a surreal change of scene arriving back at the van, changing out of ski gear and driving away into what felt like another season. It wasn't long until the land of ice and snow where we had been living was a distant view in the wing mirrors as we sped along the toll roads towards what felt like summer.

We'd agreed to meet Team Jepson at a small village called Cormot which promised cheap accommodation and great climbing for the next day. The plan was to enjoy a hearty meal and a cold beer while revelling in our ski touring success.

When we eventually rolled into the village at 22:30, all was quiet, with the shutters firmly closed on every property. Arriving first and having initially been unable to locate the hut, Clare and I were just about to set off to find somewhere to bivi for the night, when headlights approached, and Team Jepson rolled into town. Spirits rose, as they did at least know which hut was the correct one, but celebrations were soon thwarted on the discovery of it being locked up and closed along with the rest of the village.

Having run out of alternative options and given the late hour, we all decided to bivi, so we drove the short distance up to the crag car park and got ourselves established into sleep mode. We had to lend Team Jepson our 'Therm-a-Rest' sleeping mats and a large tarp to bivi on because they were not equipped for a night of camping. Ewan and Alys got first dibs on them, Dodi took the car and we zipped Tim up inside his ski bag on the floor outside, with much hilarity.

Fontainebleau, France
Milly-le-Forest Campsite (closed).

April 4th 2008

LOGBOOK ENTRY:
"Awoke to perfect blue sky in the morning and were quick to brew up some fresh coffee. Had breakfast in bed while the sun came around. There was a frost on the people bivving outside! Now packing away ski kit and repacking rucksacks with climbing gear. Going to do a route or two here in Cormot, then continue north to Fontainebleau..."

Later that day having arrived in Fontainebleau...

"Had a great day cragging at Cormot, before taking on another section of the péage. Got to Font at about 18:30 and stopped in town to take photos of the famous Chateau and eat some pizza. It was nearly 20:30 by the time we located the campsite, which was, of course, closed. We just parked up anyway on a flat sandy spot nearby. Managed to muster up the energy to make some soup before crawling into our nest of down feathers.

Three days of ski touring, one day of rock climbing and about 400 miles of driving since we last had a shower or wore some fresh clothes! Tomorrow...maybe?!"

Everyone survived the impromptu night in the Cormot car park and we felt more grateful than ever to own Therm-a-Rest mattresses to sleep on. A night sleeping in the van without them makes you realise how much comfort and warmth they actually provide. The meagre lining of Karrimat under the van carpet was not sufficient for a cold night!

"A significant crag of national importance", was how Tim sold us on the trip to Cormot on the way home. Well, that and the lure of a cheap club hut to stay in.

While the night in the hut never materialised, it was worth it for the laughs we had getting Tim zipped into his ski bag in the middle of the night. As promised, we did have a great day on the cliffs, climbing for as long as we could before getting back in the van and continuing north heading for another great climbing destination, Fontainebleau.

Boulogne, France
North Bound Service Station

April 5th 2008

LOGBOOK ENTRY:
"Service station on the toll road, just south of the Boulogne. Good climbing at Font. Sore finger-tips. Ferry back to Dover in the morning..."

Maxing out the last of our time abroad was achieved by sampling some of the world's best bouldering venues around Fontainebleau. Unfortunately, we hadn't managed to squeeze a bouldering mat into the van as well as our ski kit. The Escort is awesome, but it still has its limits!

So we spent a day seeking out low traverse boulder problems and ones that didn't pose too much danger of falling. Luckily many of the boulders have a sandy base so we were able to enjoy the area until our fingers protested and it was time to leave.

With a morning ferry booked we did our usual pitstop bivi in a service station. This time just outside of Boulogne before dashing for the ferry the next morning and driving onwards to Fort Martin for dinner.

A final alpine start the following morning, had me back in Wales in time for a 9:30 am staff meeting, having not been home since I last left work. Making the most of the holidays!

Torpoint, Cornwall
Outside Kernow HQ

June 14th - 16th 2008

LOGBOOK ENTRY:
"House renovation horror. Outgoing tenants have left some unwanted baggage - slept outside the house in the van due to a flea infestation inside. Four days of solid grafting - scrubbing mould, stripping wallpaper, throwing out carpets, painting - generally returning it to a state fit for human habitation. Too exhausted to write and don't really want to remember this hardship. Enough said."

Not all our van bivies were the start of fun adventures in the outdoors. Sometimes they were just out of necessity.

On this occasion, it was due to the grim realities of our landlord duties at our flat in Torpoint. Since moving to North Wales we had let our flat through an agent and only periodically checked in when a tenant moved on. For a while all had been well, but for reasons unknown, we were informed that the current occupiers had left without warning leaving it in a less than desirable state.

A work party, consisting of myself, Clare and my long-suffering parents, travelled down for what we hoped would be a long, but productive day, after which we'd stay in the flat, go for a celebratory meal and then return back home feeling suitably satisfied.

It didn't quite go to plan. On entering the property, it soon became clear it was in a real state - there were fleas literally jumping out of the carpet! We beat a hasty retreat to B&Q, returning dressed in newly purchased hazmat all-in-one white suits. The neighbour's net curtains soon began twitching as it looked like a forensic team were entering the scene of a crime.

There was a surprising amount of hilarity given the distressing nature of the task in hand but sleeping in the flat was definitely out of the question. Parked up next to our recently hired skip, we chose to stay in the van, while my folks retired to a room above a nearby pub. It really is bad when a night in the back of an escort van, next to a skip, is preferable to staying in an actual house!

Rouen, France
On the road to Rouen – Southbound

July 12th 2008

LOGBOOK ENTRY:
"On the toll road, en route to the south of France and beyond. Beginning of the 'Picos de Europa Summer 2008 Expedition'. Ferry delayed by four and a half hours, so instead of arriving in France at 20:00, it was gone midnight. Boo! Drove until just after 2 am, totally knackered. Slept through until 08:30, bought a coffee for a Euro (very nice too), then continued. Got to the beach at 19:00, a few kilometres north of Biarritz. Walked to water's edge for sunset. Not great surf, but a beautiful place. Got horizontal by 21:30 and slept for twelve hours undisturbed."

The first day of what ended up being a fifty-two-day van odyssey that took us through England, down the coast of France and onto the beaches and mountains of Northern Spain. With a tried and tested format for maximising our already generous holiday allowances, we would leave home at the earliest possible opportunity, usually with me in the pre-loaded van, meeting Clare minutes after she delivered her final lectures of the term, to ensure a rapid and smooth getaway. The return journey would usually have us back just in time for the new term's staff meeting.

However, this summer, we had delayed our ferry for a few days to allow us to watch a concert (Ben Folds Five), in Liverpool and swing by the family in Fort Martin.

The smooth exit from North Wales, live music, a late night, and then a relaxing day with family and friends was all panning out like the well-planned operation it was. After catching our breath, we left Fort Martin feeling excited, if a little nervous, about the coming weeks away. As we'd already learnt – flexibility is the key to success, so when the cancelled ferry signs flashed up, we took the time to have a few moments on the beach rather than waiting in the building traffic jam. After boarding a later ferry, the long drive through France passed without incident and although we arrived exhausted, it felt amazing to be on an expedition again. Simplifying life with what can be carried in the van, such as clothes, equipment and money, normal life can be put on hold, allowing us to concentrate our attention on whatever adventure might arise. It is a liberating and energising experience.

Picos de Europa, Spain
On a dirt track below Fresnidiello Slabs

July 18th 2008

LOGBOOK ENTRY:
"We're in the Picos de Europa, deep in the heart of the mountains! Somewhere along a dusty dirt road, we've found a layby underneath the imposing limestone slabs of Pena de Fresnidiello. Did the first four pitches of a climb in the evening shade. Down at the van at 21:00 for couscous and sleep. 05:45 start tomorrow for a route (1 hour walk-in time) before the sun becomes toasting (at about 09:30!). Amazing moonlit night - full. Felt as alone as any alpine bivi, but with all the luxuries of the van!"

Before our departure from home, we had not been able to glean a huge amount of information about rock climbing in the Picos de Europa; an often-overlooked National Park on the north coast of Spain. The enormous, towering spire of Naranjo de Bulnes is the centrepiece of this mountainous region. It's considered Spain's national mountain and is well known and easily identified by Spaniards, but outside of their country, its presence was almost one of a secret myth. It was clear that there was going to be plenty of climbing to keep us busy for a few months, but we'd only sourced an old guidebook from 1989 that contained any English descriptions of the routes. We had to teach ourselves how to translate Spanish route descriptions with the help of the dictionary that we carried in the 'library' section of the van.

Thanks to the UIAA (Union International Alpine Association), an internationally translatable series of symbols has been developed to denote certain climbing or physical features on a cliff, allowing topos and sketch diagrams to be read by any climber or alpinist, no matter what language they speak. Britain, for some reason, has also developed their own version, which is translatable to anyone who can read English. This had served us well in our home counties, but to become bonafide Euro climbers, we had to educate ourselves in the ways of 'route-reading' the way our foreign friends do. Despite the general dearth of information, we had found a photo and sketch topo online of the enormous limestone slabs of Pena de Fresnidiello. They looked incredible and were soon added to our itinerary in the 'must visit' section.

It is possible to get a ferry from the south coast of England, direct to the north coast of Spain, but with the Dover to Calais crossing costing a mere fraction of the price, we opted to take on the overland drive through France. Rather than beeline straight for the mountains, we decided to break up the journey by stopping at the various surf beaches of Frances' west coast. As well as the bonus of catching some great waves, we anticipated that this more relaxed pace of travel also was likely to leave both the van and its passengers in a better state to go mountaineering once we arrived in Spain.

After a week that had been interspersed with driving and surfing, we pulled into the small town of Potes on the edge of the Picos de Europa National Park. With the glistening sea behind us, we focused our attention on the enticing jagged peaks that formed the skyline in front of us. Before us lay a whole mountain range full of untold adventures to be played out over the next month or so. The excitement was palpable.

Getting to the actual cliffs was almost as nerve-racking as the ensuing climbing. As we had recently discovered, the rural Spanish roads would not always be tarmacked to a level that would be considered safe or legal in the UK. Once out of a village or hamlet, they were rarely tarmacked at all and the van didn't seem too impressed by this. We were following what looked on our map to be a fairly main road when the black asphalt gave way to white dusty gravel. Dropping the speed down to a crawl, we cautiously bumped and bounced our way up the valley, leaving a plume of dust in our slow-moving wake. With every turn, the conditions got a little bit worse and we regularly ground to a halt before deciding to 'just' have a look around the next corner. Sweating with nerves as much as the heat, we coaxed the little van further and further into what seemed to be no place for a motorised vehicle.

As the gradient levelled out, the road turned into a wide green valley that had previously been hidden from view. We each breathed out a long sigh of relief at having to go no further and in amazement at the sight that greeted us. There was no mistaking that we were in the right place. The slabs of rock that we had set out from Wales in search of, were now clear to see, high up on the other side of the valley, above the lush green meadow. They were exactly as pictured in our photograph, but here in the bright light of day, they seemed much bigger.

We were in no fit state to set off on a big rock climb and not least because the hike to the base of the climbing was an hour away. We were hot, sweaty and frazzled from the drive; the combinations of which were causing me a crushing headache. We needed shade and we needed water. Using the tarp from the van, we managed to achieve some level of comfort and rested in the remaining afternoon light, just happy not to be driving. The layby that we had pulled into would serve us well for the night, before setting out in the morning. We were well stocked with food and water and all we had to do was rest and sort the climbing kit. The road didn't look like it was going to see much else in the way of traffic for the rest of the day, so we didn't have to worry about it being a legitimate place to spend the night.

From underneath the shade of my umbrella, the views were awe-inspiring and even though my head was throbbing, it was impossible not to marvel at the views. The hidden valley that we had arrived in had a wide grassy base with a small river and was hemmed in by steep mountains on both sides. The lower valley that we had driven up from was now completely hidden from view and apart from the dirt track that we were parked alongside, there was no other trace of human presence. With the binoculars, we scanned the huge sweep of rock opposite us and managed to roughly line up some of the cracks and ledges with the features on our sketched topo to our chosen line of ascent.

We had intended to try and rest in the shade, cook up a hearty meal at dusk and then sit out the back of the van as the sun dropped below the horizon. We figured that as the light faded, the air temperature would cool to a much more pleasant level and we'd be able to lie out watching the stars and generally soak up the wilderness ambience. But later in the afternoon, despite the heat, the lure of adventure had us sweating up the opposite hillside towards the rock. It didn't take long to realise what we already knew – it was way too hot for this! It's said that real learning comes best from experiencing a situation rather than gleaning knowledge learned from a book. This seemed to be a case example – I literally can't describe the energy-zapping feeling of the sun's heat as it beat down on us that afternoon. Bathed in sweat, we arrived at the base of the cliff, where one small boulder provided salvation in the form of enough shade for us both to cower under for half an hour until the long shadows crept up from the valley to our isolated position on the hillside. With the sun gone, we could begin to think straight again.

Our reconnaissance with the binoculars earlier had paid off and we managed to locate the base of the route without too much navigational trouble, despite the absence of any real path. The rock features seemed to match up with our twenty-year-old route topo, but worryingly, there didn't seem to be any sign of any bolts up ahead to confirm our deductions. As it turned out, the game of 'hunt the start of the climb' would have to wait as there was unexpected trouble of a different kind approaching.

It was hard to register exactly what was going on at first, as the silence of the valley was gradually broken. A low humming sound was building to a feverish drone and our eyes flicked to the sky in search of aircraft. Seeing nothing and with the unidentified sound rapidly approaching, we just had time to exchange glances before the answer revealed itself. Puzzled looks were quickly replaced by ones of fear as the source of the noise was identified. A thick, black, dancing cloud of bees was approaching at speed and before we could register what was going on, the black and yellow bodies of the front runners started bouncing off us as our paths met. 'Run' we both shouted in unison, but there was nowhere to go! Above us was the smooth base of the steep rock slabs and below us, the angle was just as unattractively steep and covered in long grass.

Unable to outrun the swarm, all we could do after retreating a few panicked paces, was hit the deck at the base of a small bush. Curled up into balls, with arms over our heads we tried to be as small as possible while willing the procession to keep moving past. Thankfully, after what seemed like ages, the sound died away and the coast felt clear enough to get back up. Luckily, apart from receiving the shock of witnessing the event at such close quarters, neither of us had been stung and the danger seemed to have passed. After a bit of debate about the likelihood of another flyby, we decided to get the ropes out and get up the cliff where we kidded ourselves that we'd be out of the flight path.

Our first 'big route' in a new mountain area, in a new country and a long way from civilization, was always going to have a slightly nervy feel to it. Having already had one adrenaline-inducing experience before we'd even left the ground, we set off very cautiously. It took a pitch or two for me to get into the flow of things and I was grateful that Clare was leading the first section. The rock quality was great and as we gained height, my confidence levels also rose to allow me to soak up the exposure, views, and the high mountain ambience.

The process of climbing a rock face might be perceived as being the same wherever in the world you are, but different rock types present different features and therefore different challenges. The main rock type in the

Picos de Europa is limestone and a type that is heavily featured with water-worn runnels that have slowly eroded the rock over thousands of years. Small, positive holds and hidden pockets that could take a single finger, or large 'bucket edges' over which a whole hand or sometimes an arm can be thrown, make up the bulk of the handholds. When things get more technical, strong nerves are required as much as strong fingers, due to the necessity to balance with friction across the sloping scoops and scallops that have shaped the texture of the rock surface.

Where there are pockets and cracks to be found, protection can be placed by the leader, but across the smoother featureless terrain, concentration and a steady head were the only protection until reaching a pre-drilled bolt or peg that would provide a temporary yet comforting island of safety. As we ascended, confirmation that we were going the right way was provided in the form of a bolt, piton or sun-bleached rope thread. The bolts were placed much further apart than we would have liked them to be, so we supplemented the protection with extra gear that we were carrying. Clare was in great form and led off again up a 40m pitch containing only three bits of fixed protection before arriving at our high point.

After abseiling down the route from fixed abseil stations, we arrived back at the van in the dark. With no light pollution or moon, the sky seemed full of stars and the milky way stretched out above us while shooting stars and satellites passed overhead. It was a magical place and a fine introduction to the delights of what the Pico de Europa had to offer.

After a good night's sleep but pre-dawn, the moon had crested the mountains and the van was bathed in moonlight as we set off again from the van towards the base of the cliff. It was an incredible time of day to be moving in such a wild empty place and although we were very tired, motivation came from the desire to get to the base of the climbing while it was still cool. It was a close run race, but the sun just beat us to the base of the cliff and for a few magical moments, the whole face glowed pink.

These climbs were the beginning of an incredible van-based expedition during which we climbed, hiked and explored all around the mountains of the Picos de Europa. We were mostly interested in the long mountaineering routes up remote peaks, but we also discovered shorter climbs, extended treks and some very quirky mountain huts, including one that in a former life was the gun tower on a naval battleship. Disassembled and helicoptered into the wilderness, the metal igloo sported three bunk beds on either side of it, providing a cosy night, especially as there were a pair of resident guardians already established in two of them!

Throughout the expedition, we kept remarking on how surprising it was that there was barely any useful or well-documented information about the area in English. The area is relatively accessible from the UK and held the appeal to us that the style of climbing is mostly traditionally protected (rather than being bolted). The big difference, and attraction, was that there was a whole national park to explore, occupied by only a fraction of the visitors that flock to the more well-known alpine regions. Given that there was only one English guidebook for climbing and mountaineering in the area, by necessity, Clare had done a huge amount of research online before we left home.

On the road, we kept diligent notes and journals as we climbed and travelled through the Picos. We figured that other climbers might find this useful, so at night Clare would type these up on her laptop and shortly after our return to Wales, along with all the extensive pre-trip notes, she published a Climber's Companion (climbers-companions.com) guide to the area. The happy by-product of this idea was that the sales of the book have drip fed payments into the bank for years to come!

Fuente Dé, Spain
Fuente Dé Cable Car, Car Park

August 8th 2008

LOGBOOK ENTRY:
"The eighth day of the eighth month in two thousand and eight! Bivied in the car park at the cable car in preparation for an ascent of 'Divertimento' on the North-East Face of Pena Regaliz.

A monster three-hour walk in to get to the climb. Five hours on the route. Ten pitches of climbing, then two more hours for the return walk back down back to the van. Solid stats.

Left the van at 07:30 and returned just after 19:00! We were going to bivi again but instead drove to the campsite near Potes for showers and red wine. Amazing day. Two cheeky pitches of grade V+ (HVS, 5a) – one through an overhang and the other up long water runnels and over a bulge. We rock!"

Looking back at this logbook entry, it's partly with admiration and partly with disbelief. To hike this peak in a day would have been a respectable achievement, but to throw in a difficult and committing ten-pitch climb, gives an idea of our level of fitness, as well as the astonishing level of psych, dedication and desire for seeking out a good adventure. We have a few photos of the day, but mostly, the memories are firmly etched into our minds. From the outset, it held all the key attributes of an expedition experience, requiring us to use our skills, both physically and mentally to 'complete a journey with an unknown outcome'.

One of the main considerations when climbing and mountaineering in the Picos de Europa is ensuring the availability of drinking water. The region's limestone geology causes any rainfall to run off and disappear into the extensive network of caves that lie hidden beneath the mountains, hence the main features of the rock are water-worn runnels. While there are plenty of stream beds in the valleys, in the summer these tend to be dry as the water finds easier passage underground. We had been shown a few 'springs' and watering holes hidden in caves by locals and had a few others marked on our map, but the consensus seemed to be that they should not be relied on. The long and short of these snippets of local information was that, for any journey, hydration needs to be considered and planned for. On this occasion, the ascent involved us carrying over five litres of water to ensure that we stayed hydrated. A not insignificant additional weight to anyone's rucksack, but a necessary one.

It's a zig-zagging track of 800m altitude gain to get to the meadows of Vega de Lourdes – unless, of course, you want to pay for a lift in the nearby cable car. The financial debate was tossed back and forth, but while we would have liked to have had some mechanical assistance, the decision was taken out of our hands, as the service turned out to be closed for maintenance. The ascent was going to cost us in sweat rather than Euros.

Not that anywhere was particularly busy that summer, but the closure of the cable car meant the absence of almost any tourists or climbers in the high mountains that day. Except of course the few who were both willing and able to access them like us, via paying the obligatory 800m of height gain 'toll'.

We felt like we were the only people in the entire mountain range. Wild horses, cows, goats and 'Rebeccos' (Cantabrian chamois) roamed around the surprisingly green pastures as we hiked across them towards our peak. By now, we were getting used to the style of climbing and having previously written this climb off as too big, too difficult and too far away, our tally of recent climbs had now provided enough in the way of experience and confidence to be making an attempt. We couldn't have asked for a better day and our early start meant that we had plenty of time, fine weather, and the route to ourselves.

The first few sections were worryingly steep for the advertised grades, but we managed to keep our heads together and after four good pitches of climbing arrived at the 'Grand Terrace', where an escape was possible if required. With the knowledge that we could abort at this point we had a good psychological boost when setting off, but having arrived unscathed, we decided that we both felt 'in the zone' and having come this far should continue upwards. Refreshed by a sip of the precious water rations and a flapjack, that's exactly what we did.

The higher pitches provided some breath-taking balance moves, relying solely on the friction of our climbing shoes, but the protection was generally good, so our confidence remained buoyant. Pulling through the crux overhang involved the kind of exposed position that really ought to have warranted bringing a photographer along with us, we joked. We were both experiencing the kind of flow state that climbers, performers, or athletes aim to be in. With the level of challenge remaining high and the exposure wild, we seemed to be climbing on autopilot. Every handhold seemed to be just where we imagined it would be and each cam or wire we selected to slot into any given crack was the perfect fit and was placed without fuss. It was climbing bliss.

The final difficult pitch fell to Clare to lead, and I paid out the ropes as she disappeared over an overlap. Things began to slow down after a while, but little by little the ropes inched through my belay device until after a tense few minutes of inactivity, there was a jerk on the ropes and a 'whoop' drifted down from somewhere high above. I was more than grateful for the tight rope as I followed up the drainpipe of a water feature. Without much in the way of handholds, the rope led me past our whole rack of cams up an ever-decreasing-sized runnel. It was a stunning lead which led me up to a justifiably happy Clare, who was sat beaming, pulling up the ropes, and me, onto the summit.

Having spent the day on the shady northeast face of the mountain, my eyes squinted into the bright light of the summit. More food and drink were consumed as we sat there gazing contentedly at the multitude of horizon lines around us. Somewhere below us was a van with our bed in it.

Picos de Europa, Spain
On the jeep track, just outside the village of Sotres

August 11th 2008

LOGBOOK ENTRY:
"Very misty outside. A bit damp in the air. A really good, flat and quiet area on the bend in the track – which thankfully has recently been resurfaced (van much happier about being up here!). Major deliberations as to whether or not we should attempt to walk up to the Urelliu Hut tomorrow to try and climb the Naranjo Tower the next day when there is only one day of okay(ish) weather forecast!? Oh, the dilemmas! Should we risk it..?"

Like many mountaineers, weighing up a decision on the perceived scales of risk versus reward is a habitual pastime of mine and one of the unique factors that make our pursuits so intoxicating. Although the ultimate decision comes down to, as The Clash would speculate, "should I stay or should I go?", the calculations required to get there involve an infinite number of variables that currently no app or calculator can compute. Add to this some time to ponder the outcome, and the answer rarely comes down to a quick yes or no. Some might argue that the longer the time spent pondering, the more obstacles one is likely to think about. Certainly, in the kayaking world, there is a saying that the time one spends studying a rapid that they are about to run is directly proportionate to the time they are likely to spend swimming down it, having capsized through overthinking.

So, there we were, sitting in the back of the van, on the side of a dirt road on a misty mountainside. Somewhere up above us was the most famous peak in Spain and one of the most coveted climbs in the entire Picos de Europa mountain range. Tempting and tantalizing.

We'd woken early from a good night's sleep in the back of the van to find the surrounding hillside enveloped in a thick, damp mist. Pushing the doors open to get a look around, we soon withdrew back inside, as whatever our decision would be, there was going to be no need to make an early start. It didn't look like the heat of the sun would be a problem today. Having already snuggled back down to sleep for a few more hours, a decision was eventually going to have to be made. Should we take the gamble of a four-hour trek up to the hut in hopes of an improvement in the weather? The last forecast we'd seen had suggested there might be a slight improvement for the next morning, but after that, there were at least three or four days of poor weather on the way. It seemed like this was going to be the only weather window available to us and even though it was an unhelpfully small one, having come this far we decided we should at least give it a try.

On one hand, it felt like a real gamble, but for some reason, we felt sure we'd be lucky. With bags packed and waterproofs on, we began the slow trudge uphill on the rutted track that led to the hut some thousand metres higher above us on the mountainside. After an hour of uphill sweating on the steep muddy switchbacks of an old farm road, we were somewhat dismayed to find a load of cars had cheekily driven up and parked to start their walk from there.

We weren't convinced that a reduction in walk time was worth the risk of taking on the drive, but others clearly thought otherwise. If we hadn't seen the cars with our own eyes, I don't think that we'd have believed it possible to drive a Fiat 500 along the ground that we had just travelled over on foot. Although part of us was gutted that we'd added an extra hour onto an already big hike, we consoled ourselves with the fact that the van (and our insurance for that matter) would probably not have been too happy about us driving up the last bits of this old dirt track.

From the unofficial car park/abandonment zone, we continued upwards to where the views should have been stunning, but deep in the heart of the clouds, our visibility was limited to about ten metres. Points of interest were limited to crossing a field full of large cows and diligently spotting the odd flower. The reduced visibility meant that we could have been almost anywhere. Lost in our thoughts, we plodded onwards and upwards into the misty morning without much to describe, except to say that it was hot, sweaty, damp and tiring. The motivation that kept us going was the hope that we might ascend through and above the clouds as we had done on previous occasions, as is typical in this region.

After three and a quarter hours, the shape of the hut suddenly loomed out of the mist. There was still no sign of the fabled tower but we knew it must be somewhere close behind it. We signed in and ordered some hot water to make some cappuccinos and settled into an afternoon of card games interspersed with breaks to look outside and check on the weather (which didn't change). Even though I was not working as an International Mountain Leader, the presence of my ID card seemed to delight the guardian of the Refugio, who opened a heavily discounted tab for us as we talked for a while about our various expeditions and van travels.

Just before sunset, the cloud began to clear and we got a first glimpse of the tower. It was enormous. With necks craning skyward, we could see the impossibly steep, 600-metre smooth west face, which rears up behind the hut and for a while, the clouds descended below us for long enough to sit with the guidebook and pick out some of the routes on the face. It was both intimidating and awe-inspiring in the glow of the evening light.

While there was a bit of visibility, we also checked out the location of the path that would lead us, weather permitting, around to the south face where we intended to make our ascent the next day. By the time darkness fell, the mist had covered the west face again and we were left to go to bed with fingers crossed, for a brighter start to the day. With an alarm set for 06:15, we got into our bunks ready for a night of anticipation, with my good ear firmly on the pillow to save listening to the nearby snoring Spaniards.

Discouragingly, it was still dark and misty outside when the alarm went off, but we decided to go for it and hoped that we could end up above the clouds if we climbed high enough. A few other climbers moved around while we ate a breakfast of cereal bars, alone and by torchlight. As we left the hut, a tantalizing break in the cloud revealed a ridge of rock for a few minutes before swirling mists rolled back and hid the view again. There was just enough light to negate the need for head torches but thanks to the fog, the visibility remained at only a few metres. Quickly and quietly, the rocky path led us upwards around the north and east sides of the tower.

Our rucksacks were fairly light as we'd left our overnight kit in the hut. At a campsite in Arenas a few days previously, we'd bumped into a friend of ours who had been my mentor during my teacher training back in Wales. He also happened to be an excellent rock climber, who was famed for climbing some of the boldest and most technically difficult routes around. Being able to keep your cool, while climbing on tiny handholds, far above any scant forms of protection, at or near the limit of your ability, takes a special kind of person and Nick was exactly that. Apart from catching the occasion glint in his eye that hinted at his unique mania and magic, he's generally quite an unassuming bloke. Like many of the elite-level climbers that we knew, they were too busy getting on and climbing things rather than talking themselves up to others.

It transpired that he'd just returned from guiding some students up our intended route, so we quizzed him on what we should take on our ascent. Luckily, knowing Nick and his extraordinary abilities, we could take his advice with a pinch of salt. Having trimmed down our climbing rack to what we deemed to be an acceptable balance of weight and safety, we laid it out by the van for his perusal. "Hmm", he said, "seems a bit of a lot to carry in my opinion". When pressed as to what he had taken to guide the route, he replied that he'd just taken a couple of HMS karabiners for the belays and a few lightweight quickdraws. Slightly aghast, yet knowing that he probably wasn't even exaggerating, we decided to shoulder the extra weight to benefit from a slightly greater margin of safety. Although his gear advice was a bit off-kilter, he did give us some helpful knowledge about the route, which eased our nerves and boosted our confidence.

As we reached the col below the east face and almost without warning, we suddenly broke through the cloud layer into the glory of a magic mountain moment. Rising in front of us, in crystal clear clarity, was the majestic and enormous east face, while our feet felt like they were stepping onto the surface of a sea of clouds. The timing was perfect, as the sun was just coming over the horizon to bathe the rock in an orange glow, reflecting all kinds of colours onto the top of the clouds. It was a beautiful moment to be alive and created a sensory overload that stopped us in our tracks.

A little bit further saw us into the shade at the base of the south face where it didn't take long to locate the start of our climb. Following Nick's advice, a short scramble through some slabs got us to the start of the technical climbing, at which point we noticed that there was a guide with some clients emerging from the clouds who looked hot on our heels. But apart from them, there was no one else in sight and the mountain was ours. Keen not to get stuck behind them, in a flash, Clare had the ropes uncoiled and was gearing up ready to go. The guide was really helpful and chatted with us while he sorted his clients and pointed us in the right direction. With the knowledge that the other team were waiting to climb, Clare flew up the first and the hardest of the pitches in a matter of minutes and soon the ropes came tight - my signal to climb.

The sun, although close, was still half an hour away from hitting the south face and my hands were frozen solid which was in stark contrast to our previous climbing adventures that had until now, mostly been hampered by the extreme heat. Up here, I was dressed in multiple layers of fleece, a hat and a waterproof jacket and yet still my hands were completely numb as I fumbled my way up to Clare. A new climbing technique had to be employed, which involved clamping my feelingless hands onto the holds and jamming them into cracks in the hope that they would stay in place. There was no time for hand warming once I reached Clare's belay stance, as the group had already set off below us. A quick swap of the kit was all that was allowed before I was off again.

The climbing was relatively straight forward but I found myself putting in extra gear as I was worried that my hands might betray me unless they were curled firmly around a huge hold. The thought of climbing the pitch, armed only with a couple of quickdraws and karabiners, as per Nick's advice, was beyond outrageous to me. My digits stayed cold, but as fast as I could I climbed the 40 metre pitch and found the next belay. From here, Clare kept the speed on and led through the next pitch hardly even stopping at my hanging stance. The guide reached me just as I was leaving and we were suitably chuffed when he called up to say "whoa, you two are fast"! The compliment served to spur us on, and from there, we left them for dust.

The position and climbing were magnificent as we flew through pitch after pitch. The last three rope lengths were easy scrambling, but we decided to stay roped up as we were now well over 200 metres above the ground. When at last I pulled onto the summit ridge, I peered over the edge and could see, quite literally, straight down the other side of the mountain. We took off the ropes for the final easy ground of the ridge scramble that led us to the summit where a small carving of a Madonna marked the highest point. Brilliant! Alone on the summit! What a feeling!

The views were incredible, but the feeling inside was even better. It felt like all our previous climbs had led up to this moment. Our elation was temporarily quashed when we found that the cold had drained the camera battery of its power and that in our rush, we'd left the spare one in our bag at the bottom of the climb. Luckily, by taking the battery out and warming it up in our hands we managed to get it to work and a summit selfie was salvaged.

The effort of making an early start was paying off now, as it was almost an hour that we spent alone on the top before the guided party arrived. After he'd pointed out a few peaks and notable landmarks for us, as well as the coastline we'd soon be surfing at, we left the guide and his team so they could have the same solitary summit experience as us. Scrambling carefully down the gully from the summit ridge, we located the all-important first abseil station, to begin the descent.

After the first two abseils, we came across a team of three guys who were also abseiling the same way down. We had not seen them near the summit so assumed they must have been up super early to get to the top before us. As we joined them on the small stance, they didn't appear to be too slick with their ropework and rather than hold us up they said that we should overtake. As we bypassed their ropes, they spoke a little bit of broken English to us and explained that they had spent the night on the summit. "Wow, brilliant," said Clare "that sounds really exciting!". Their faces seemed to tell a different story though, and it transpired that it was not a planned night out. Due to the bad weather and with darkness falling before they could find their way down they had been benighted! Without shelter, food or water they had survived the night on half a packet of cigarettes but left us assured that they would now make it down without assistance. We continued to the ground and after collecting our bags, walked away from any danger of stone fall before sitting back to admire the view of the south and east faces.

The benighted team safely reached the ground half an hour later and stumbled over to us, where we tried to cheer them up by giving them a well-received refill from our water bottles to help them get back to the hut. And then, as if on cue, the clouds began to lift from the valley and the tower of rock slowly became consumed, disappearing from view again, as the weather window began to close. Taking care to locate the small rock cairns that marked the path, in a thick mist we all made our way back to the refuge of the hut. More good news greeted us after a celebratory cup of herbal tea, as when I tried to pay for our stay, they insisted that as 'mountaineering professionals', we owed them nothing except that we leave with a handshake and the assurance that I would return with clients again one day.

Hossegor, France
Pin Sec Surf Camp

August 18th 2008

LOGBOOK ENTRY:
"Insanely busy! Campsites everywhere are all booked solid. Traffic chaos to add to the fun (and it's virtually raining). Checked into a full campsite, which had found us a 'place', but it was about 2m² and surrounded by tents on three sides and the toilet block on the other. In the end, we just got them to find us somewhere flat where we could park, cook up and go to sleep. They still charged us €26.50 for the privilege. Cowboys! Got straight out after breakfast. Daylight robbery."

The difference between travelling in and out of the holiday season could not have been starker. What, at the start of summer was a cheap and idyllic peaceful place to rest for a few days, had been transformed into more of a theme park than a campsite and the busiest place we'd been all expedition. If we could have gone elsewhere then we would have, but out of options and energy, we were reluctantly forced to stay the night. We'd stopped her on our journey across to the Picos and it had been a quiet idyllic spot but we should have known that at some point, the empty open-air disco, restaurants and other entertainment, must be there for a reason. It's clearly an enjoyable way to spend the summer holidays for some – just not us.

The southwest coast of France does have some great surf beaches and since we still had a bit of time as well as surfboards with us, all we needed was an agreeable place to stay. A map from the nearby tourist office provided the perfect solution. After explaining that we didn't need a laundrette, mini-mart or crazy golf facilities, a 'camping rural' site was recommended. It was only a few minutes to drive to the coast, but away from the more popular and therefore busy beaches. On the edge of a sleepy French village, was a small field with a couple of caravans in-situ. It was the polar opposite of the horrors of the previous night and ideal for two weary travellers to make a home for the week, quietly rest, recuperate and catch some waves.

The van seemed to need the rest as much as we did after being put through its paces in the challenging terrain of the Picos de Europa. To be fair, by now, the van was performing much better, but that's mostly after receiving some emergency surgery somewhere in the heart of rural northern Spain. The bad luck of experiencing a full-on breakdown was countered with the good luck of it happening at one of the cheapest and best campgrounds that we came across in the entire trip.

For reasons that are still unknown, the small village of Bonar is home to a disproportionately large municipal campsite. The campsite had three qualities that were all particularly appealing to us. The first was its relative proximity to one of the best, yet almost completely unknown single-pitch bolted crags in the Picos. Second, despite containing almost no facilities, (just a bar and a small shower block), it did house an Olympic-sized, open-air swimming pool. And the third was that it was so cheap to stay there, it was basically free!

Employing the tactic of travelling with the windows down and heaters on was fairly standard procedure that summer, but arriving in Bonar, things had begun to reach a new level of under-bonnet heat, with temperatures that didn't seem to shift even at night. At times, we had to pull over to let things cool down before gingerly pressing on at low speed. Eventually, the white flag of surrender was waved in the form of an alarming amount of dashboard illumination flashing into life to warn us of imminent engine doom. We rolled into this particular campsite and ground to a halt behind the smoking bonnet. Naturally, this happened on a Friday, so any sort of rescue would not be available until the following Monday!

An enforced weekend of larking about in the big swimming pool ensued. The pool was fabulous and mostly unfrequented. There was a very relaxed vibe around it except for one inexplicable rule – hats must be worn. You could run on the side, dive, bomb, shout and scream, or wear long shorts, short shorts or a skimpy thong, but it was a massive social faux pas, to attempt to enter the water without a regulation red and white hat! We happily donned them, grateful that there wasn't the classic European enforced 'speedos' law as well.

The day of 'van recovery' started earlier than usual and with an alarm going off to ensure that we were ready and waiting by nine in case the insurance company rang to say that our breakdown truck was on its way. Bear in mind that this was 2008 and international phone calls to a mobile were staggeringly expensive and a total last resort so missing a call was not an option. Luckily, as promised, before the weekend, the company organised a very nice man (Harry), to pick us up and take us to the nearest Ford garage.

It was all rather exciting and certainly seemed to be giving the other campers some entertainment while eating their breakfasts. With the van carefully loaded onto the bright yellow rescue truck, we were ushered to climb on board and were soon driving away. Our man Harry didn't speak much English, but he was full of smiles and made a real effort to communicate with us during the journey, which was quite sweet, as well as kind. He could just as easily have driven us there in silence, but he did his best to tell us about the nearby mines that he used to work in, where he lived and possibly that he was really into bird spotting. It is amazing what you can get across without any common language.

Away from the village, there seemed to be nothing but barren dusty land and uninhabited mountains that gave little indication of civilization, let alone a Ford dealership. Much to our surprise, like an oasis in the desert, after about 30 kilometres, an enormous blue Ford sign appeared in the distance. It was hard to believe, but it did appear to be a proper Ford garage. Our tow man Harry had warmed to us on the journey because instead of just ditching us once we got there, he hung around and said he wanted to keep an eye on the garage workers because they seemed to be "making a small problem into a big one". He was worried they were going to try and take advantage of the hapless Brits, so he did all the talking to the mechanics for us and then made the effort to translate it to us through patient guesswork and signing. What a nice guy.

Anyway, amazingly, after some tense moments, they decided that they did have the part we needed in stock and everything seemed to be well. So Harry took his leave and we paid up the negotiated seventy-two euros. No receipt was forthcoming, but we couldn't understand the explanation of why. It did seem a bit strange, but everything else about the place was very officially 'Ford' right down to the plastic bag they gave us the old parts in, but hey-ho, seventy-two euros seemed an okay fee to get the little old Escort van, and us, back on the road.

We were just relieved to be moving again without having incurred too much of a loss of time or money. On the way back to the campsite, we made a short stop to access the internet before returning to our pool for a much-needed cooldown. The trip was back on, but only after a bit more brilliant jumping, diving, somersaulting, swimming and underwater acrobatics – with hats on of course.

During our final week on the French coast, our rest and recuperation at the rural campsite got a little railroaded when we chanced upon a surf and music festival at the nearby Rip Curl Pro competition. Good times, live music and late nights ensued after watching some pros get towed out to enormous waves by jet skis. We happily spectated from the safety of the beach when things got really big but were able to ride our own waves once things calmed down.

We set off north the following week, feeling very happy, but as is usually the sign of any good expedition or adventure, more tired than when we'd arrived. It was time to go home for a rest.

On the road...

Afterword...

The Escort van travels continued for plenty of more years to come (see the 'further travels' section at the end of the book to get a feel for some of the other places the poor van managed to transport us). In doing so, it's visited at least fourteen European countries, several of these multiple times, along with proving itself to be a workhorse in other ways while at home.

When not being driven or slept in, it was used for house removals, shifting building supplies, loading logs for the fire, as a first driving lesson for one of my international students, as a beachside changing room for surfers, a storage facility for outdoor gear and a place to brew a cuppa when the weather was bad. In April 2013, it even served as our Wedding car!

All good things are said to come to an end and in December 2013, with some time away from the UK beckoning, we decided rather reluctantly, that the time had come to sell the van. The Escort (aka 'The Cessna') had been our trusted companion on countless adventures over the years, as documented in the pages of this book.

We were the second owners when we got it, and the mileage when we said goodbye stood at just over 170,000 miles, so it's fair to say that we had pretty good value from it. But to leave it on the driveway during our impending four-month sabbatical might just have been the end of it - much better to pass it on and let the wheels keep turning with someone else.

The Cessna is now gone but the memories remain.

The start of another journey...
Photo: M. Lyons

Further Van Logbook Entries

And perhaps the contents page of the Van Bivi Logbook Part Two...

Llangollen, Wales
Wern Isaf Farm (below Trevor Rocks)

October 18th -19th 2008

LOGBOOK ENTRY:
"Ian and Clare's North Wales mini-break! A little climbing road trip to avoid the bad weather in the mountains. Climbed at Trevor Rocks, World's End and then at Nesscliffe, before returning home via the Llanberis Slate Quarry. Clare led 'sterling Silver' E2 (5c)**. Great to get away and be out climbing, but boy does it get dark early!"

Aviemore, Scotland
Rothimurchus Visitors Centre Car Park

January 30th 2009

LOGBOOK ENTRY:
"On the solo. Ian. Association of Mountaineering Instructors AGM at Glenmore Lodge. Barely any snow in the glens, but okay climbing condition in the corries."

Luxemburg
Service Station somewhere en route to Switzerland

April 5th 2009

LOGBOOK ENTRY:
"Heading to the Albula Alps, in Eastern Switzerland. Very comfy night, with skis stashed overhead. Bed at midnight after Norfolk Line crossing to Dunkirk. Back on the road at 7 am, with coffee and croissants. Beauty weather - looks like summer around here rather than ski touring conditions. Hopefully snow will appear?!."

Boulogne, France
Service Station near Ferry Terminal (northbound)

April 20th 2009

LOGBOOK ENTRY:
"The return journey and a night at the usual service station. Ferry strike up ahead! Boulogne is like a refugee camp! Free tea, coffee and fruit are being handed out by the Red Cross (Croix Rouge actually), so no complaints from us.
As it turned out, we only had a short delay as things cleared up soon after our arrival."

Pembroke, Wales
Bosherton

October 27th 2009

LOGBOOK ENTRY:
"Long, long drive down the coast road from North Wales. The plan was to stop and surf at Borth but big dumping waves onto a rocky beach did not appeal. Went for a beach walk, south of Aberystwyth then carried on reaching Bosherton village just after 18:00.
Unsurprisingly, in late October, the campsite (basically someone's back garden) was deserted. Cooked up in the dark (clocks went back a few days ago), then spent the evening eating, drinking, reading, eating some more

and playing a dice words game. Then checked guidebooks for tomorrow's plan.
Now it's raining quite hard. It should all be gone by the morning!? Really mild weather. Almost hot in fact, which is very strange."

Reading, England
Snowbound on a BP Petrol Station forecourt

December 22nd 2009

LOGBOOK ENTRY:
"Christmas escape plans almost foiled by heavy snow! Stuck in Reading, unable to reach the Airport! Winter traffic chaos gripping the streets much harder than the slippery snow!"

Stanage, Peak District, England
North Lees Farm

May 16th 2010

LOGBOOK ENTRY:
"Clare's Birthday Mini-Break! Drove straight to the Peak District after a day's work open boating on the River Dee. Super good to be back in Van Bivi mode. Blue skies, a big van cook-up, a bottle of beer and a comfy duvet! Not a DIY tool or paintbrush in sight! We love our new Cottage, but it's great to have a break!"

Stanage, Peak District, England
North Lees Farm Campsite

May 17th 2010

LOGBOOK ENTRY:
"Another fine day of climbing Gritstone classics at Stanage Edge. Van bivi back at North Lees after hot showers and fine food. Clare's last day of 28

years tomorrow – aiming to climb 28-star points worth of routes during this Peaks trip.
Hathersage stop on the way home for shops, coffee and chilling on a sunny café terrace. Beauty."

Glan Conwy, Wales
Layby near River Conwy

June 12th 2010

LOGBOOK ENTRY:
"Partied in Liverpool until very late, celebrating 40 Years of Outdoor Education at I.M.Marsh! Drove back west to Glan Conwy, slept in a layby nearby the estuary. In work by 09:15 for 'brunch' and summited Tryfan at 13:00! All in a day's work!"

Lake District, England
Burn's Farm, Near Keswick

October 27th – 28th 2010

LOGBOOK ENTRY:
"Half-term climbing tour. Arrived after dark (without rear lights on the van) after a few routes at Trowbarrow Quarry – a cliff that surely must collapse soon. Thursday started with an ascent of 'Little Chamonix' at Shepherds Crag before rain stopped play. Great to be enjoying a bit of van life – even if it's thundering outside! Burn's campsite - £5.00 each. Crackin'."

Hawkshead, Lake District
Town Centre Campsite

October 29th 2010

LOGBOOK ENTRY:
"Prolonged and heavy rain. Walked to Alcock Tarn below Heron Pike, before returning to Ambleside for shelter in the form of shops, cinema and pizza."

Pitlochery, Scotland
Layby No.41 on A9 (northbound)

January 28th 2011

LOGBOOK ENTRY:
"First bivi of 2011! Finished a day's climbing work followed by parents' evening, and then started driving. Was in the zone and went non-stop all the way here! Adam and Paul are now both parked up behind me having arrived later during the night (I arrived at midnight). Carried on to Drumochter the next morning and climbed a few peaks, including Beinn Udlamain (1011m), then continued onto Glenmore Lodge for the Association of Mountaineering Instructors AGM. Bed just after 1 am..."

Kingusse, Scotland
Layby on the A9 (southbound)

January 31st 2011

LOGBOOK ENTRY:
"The return leg! Tired. Climbed Ewan Buttress (Grade III/IV) in Corie nan Lochan in the Cairngorms with Adam. Good route, but dropped crampon off the second pitch! (fell off my boot somehow?). Had to cut steps to finish the pitch! Abseiled off and recovered it from the snow slopes below (after the stuck ropes incident). Adam then fell on the walkout, breaking his walking pole, then later broke a crampon prong! What a day! Oh and all that, with a 75mph wind. Phew."

Tregarth, North Wales
Dinas Farm

May 14ᵗʰ 2011

LOGBOOK ENTRY:
"Bronze Duke of Edinburgh's Award Training Expedition Camp. A dismal day of torrential rain showers, lost groups and wet boots eventually ended with all pupils here at the campsite. I need to go and meet a different group tomorrow, so by no small amount of good fortune, I've suddenly found myself with a van to bivi in! The joy! Oh and I've managed to leave my waterproof coat at home. Brilliant. A spacious night's sleep, spoilt only by the 7 am alarm clock."

Duddon Valley, Lake District
Wallabarrow Farm

June 1ˢᵗ 2011

LOGBOOK ENTRY:
"Drove up from The Cottage this afternoon. Nice coffee stop at 'The Swan Hotel' at Newby Bridge at the end of Lake Windermere. Did a route called 'Thomas' (Severe) on Wallabrrow Crag and now cooking up a Rosti and sippin' a beer in the back of the van. Holiday-tastic."

Langdale, Lake District
Baysbrown Farm

June 4ᵗʰ 2011

LOGBOOK ENTRY:
"Lake District Tropicana continues! Phew, what a scorcher! Esk Buttress (and swims in the deep turquoise plunge pools) on Friday, Raven Crag ticked today. Wow! Great days and some dream building in the van to top it off!"

Llangurig, Mid-Wales
Layby in the middle of nowhere

June 14th 2011

LOGBOOK ENTRY:
"En route to a Duke of Edinburgh's Award meeting in Llandovery. Set off from The Cottage last night at 22:00 to break up the journey. Ultimate comfort but blue sky today – typical for an indoor meeting schedule. Clare reporting good surf conditions from back up north!"

Llandudno, North Wales
St David's College

June 29th 2011

LOGBOOK ENTRY:
"Am bivied outside the expedition stores in preparation for tomorrow's '3 Peaks Challenge' attempt. Alarm clock is set for only four hours time! Ugh! Cader Idris, Tryfan and Snowdon await..."

Lyon, France
Service Station near Lyon (southbound)

July 14th 2011

LOGBOOK ENTRY:
"The Cessna is back in Europe! The thumbs up from Pandy Motors in Tregarth has set us on another Alpine Odyssey! Bivied at a service station near Lyon. Great bivi! Super comfy, loads of room and even have fresh sheets and duvet! Brilliant! Croissants and coffee in the morning made us even happier."

Calais, France
Service Station near Calais (northbound)

August 18th 2011

LOGBOOK ENTRY:
"Another summer of fun draws to an end. Alpine adventures finished with a five-star break in Perigueux with Clare's Mum and Bob. Drove from 14:30 to 23:15. At ferry terminal now, then onwards to Fort Martin for the weekend."

Peak District, England
Camp near Hathersage

October 27th 2011

LOGBOOK ENTRY:
"Arrived in darkness at 21:00 (because we left late having booked flights to Turkey for Christmas and stopped off at Cheshire Oakes). We were aiming for Hathersage but pulled off into a Caravan Park about ten minutes out. Flat ground. Quiet. Just right. Pasta, Tuborg and bed. I was toasty, but Clare was up in the night in search of power stretch fleece and Smartwool socks. Woke at 9 am. 8°C and thick, thick mist. No need to rush to the crags, so are now on our second cup of tea in bed. About to cook porridge and now the clouds are starting to part. Aiming for Bamford Edge..."

Hathersage, Peak District
North Lees Farm

October 28th - 29th 2011

LOGBOOK ENTRY:
"Cragging. Burbidge North."

Aviemore, Scotland
Café Car Park

January 3rd 2012

LOGBOOK ENTRY:
"Nine and a half hours of driving from North Wales. At one point, I ended up driving south on the M6 due to roadworks! Blizzards near Glasgow. Snowing so hard as I crossed the Dromocher Pass that I did not dare stop, so carried on to Aviemore and pulled into the café car park. The start of three weeks of MIC training."

Ballachulish, Scotland
Edge of the petrol station forecourt

January 20th 2012

LOGBOOK ENTRY:
"My winter residence at The Alex Mac hut was fully booked, so had to move out for the night! Had some dinner and a shower, drove down the road for a sleep, and then came back for breakfast at 06:30! Super windy – van rocking all night long."

Llandudno, Wales
St David's College Car Park

July 1st 2012

LOGBOOK ENTRY:
"In preparation for a 3:30 am start. Alarm set and sadly it's already nearly midnight. Alpine bliss is only a few days away now though. Three Peaks Challenge time again! Cader Idris climbed at 08:04, Tryfan at 14:06 and Snowdon summit reached at 19:03. Back at The Cottage at midnight."

Paris, France
Service Station (southbound)

August 14th 2012

LOGBOOK ENTRY:
"Paris – by mistake! On our way to visit Clare's Mum and go surfing. Tricky navigation, a closed ring road and an inappropriate map were just some of the factors that suddenly found us driving through the centre of Paris at midnight (a fact confirmed by several easily identifiable local landmarks). Took a very low tunnel under the city and saw the Arch de Triumph and Eiffel Tower all illuminated and up close. Eventually found our way out and bivied at a service station just south of the city. 5 hours the next day got us to Perigueux."

Calais, France
Service Station (northbound)

August 27th 2012

LOGBOOK ENTRY:
"Drove up from Trappes after an amazing weekend in Paris (this time on purpose, involving hotels and fine living). Slept at the end of the toll roads. Eurotunnel awaits at 08:05 tomorrow and then onward travel to The Cottage, via Fort Martin."

Notes
Summer Trip Mileage:
10/07/12 = 147279
02/09/12 = 149751

Edale, Peak District
Edale Campsite

November 2nd 2012

LOGBOOK ENTRY:
"Arrived late from Wales. Kinder explorations. Coffee and croissants set us up for an ascent of Crowden Brook, onto Kinder and Grindslow Knoll. Then over to Hathersage."

Hathersage, Peak District
North Lees Farm

November 3rd 2012

LOGBOOK ENTRY:
"Morning frost on the van! Inside on the windscreen! Beautiful cloud inversion from the top of Stanage. Then back to The Cottage. Perfect little getaway. Plus, Clare got some amazing lime green Patagonia Ski Pants for our honeymoon."

Llandudno, North Wales
St David's College Expedition Stores

July 3rd 2013

LOGBOOK ENTRY:
"Outside the Expedition Store once again. How time flies. 03:55 alarm this year. 3 Peaks Challenge. Was walking up Cader Idris by 6 am. Soaked to the skin by 06:30. Arrived back here at the van at 22:45. A long, long day."

Ribble Valley, Clitheroe, UK
The Beat-Herder Festival

July 6th & 7th 2013

LOGBOOK ENTRY:
"The van provides enviable coolness from the sweltering heat! Tent-dwellers were forced outside by 07:30, while I slept peacefully until 11:30 am! A ridiculous weekend with the Liverpool JMU Alumni. Fully togged up in tweed hunting outfits, complete with water pistols and a stag to hunt. Beyond tired at the end of the weekend. Delirious in fact. Drove Matt home to Wales in a daze on Monday and the holidays have started..."

About the Author

Expeditions, travel and general outdoor adventures have been a central part of Ian Martin's life so far. After a brief pause from university studies, to remove and recover from an astonishingly large (and unwanted) brain tumour, he has made an unorthodox living and career from hanging off cliffs, climbing mountains and leading expeditions.

Inspired by wild places and those who explore them, the prospect of experiencing his own adventures drew him from his native flatlands of Northamptonshire into the transient world of expedition leadership and outdoor education. After discovering that it was possible to get paid to go rock climbing, there was no turning back.

Being immersed in the world of mountaineering and rock climbing has provided fine excuses for taking part in expeditions and world travel involving all modes of transport – not just Escort Vans. He is a qualified International Mountain Leader and a Winter Climbing and Mountaineering Instructor, which together represent the highest level of mountaineering qualifications in the United Kingdom.

Further Reading

If you've enjoyed this, then take a moment to browse through my blog at www.mountainlifestyle.co.uk

It's my online resource for documentation, motivation and inspiration, with details of further climbs, expeditions and current adventures.

Home Sweet Home in the Ecrins National Park, France
Photo: A. Leary

Printed in Great Britain
by Amazon